CHILDREN TELL STORIES

A TEACHING GUIDE

Martha Hamilton & Mitch Weiss
Beauty & the Beast Storytellers

RICHARD C. OWEN PUBLISHERS, INC.
Katonah, New York

Library of Congress Cataloging-in-Publication Data

Hamilton, Martha.
 Children tell stories : a teaching guide / Martha Hamilton, Mitch
Weiss.
     p.   cm.
 Includes bibliographical references.
 ISBN 0-913461-20-2
 1. Storytelling.   2. Children's stories—Study and teaching.
I. Weiss, Mitch.   II. Title.
LB1042.H33   1990
372.6'42—dc20   90-32955
                                                       CIP

ISBN: 0-913461-20-2

    Grateful acknowledgment is made to the following for permission to reprint pre-
viously published material:
    Byrd Baylor for the story "Coyote and the Money Tree" from *And It Is Still That
Way*. Copyright © 1976 by Byrd Baylor, available from Trails West Publishing (P. O.
Box 8619, Sante Fe, NM 87504-8619; originally published by Scribner, 1976. Used by
permission of author.
    Joseph Bruchac for the story "The Brave Woman and the Flying Head," from
Iroquois Stories. Copyright © 1985 by Joseph Bruchac. Used by permission of author.
    Kay Chorao for the story "The Boy Who Turned Himself into a Peanut" from *The
Baby's Storybook*. Copyright © 1985 by Kay Chorao. Used by permission of author.
    Curtis Brown, Ltd., for the story "How Rabbit Lost His Tail" from *The Illustrated
Book of American Folklore* by Ben Botkin and Carl Withers. Reprinted by permission of
Curtis Brown, Ltd. Copyright © 1958 by B.A. Botkin.
    Rose Dobbs for the story "The Foolish Dragon" from *Once Upon a Time: Twenty
Cheerful Tales to Read and Tell*. Selected, edited, and sometimes retold by Rose
Dobbs. Copyright © 1950 by Random House, Inc. Copyright © renewed 1977 by Rose
Dobbs. Reprinted by permission of the author; and for the story "The Miser" from *More*
(*continued on p. 202*)

RICHARD C. OWEN PUBLISHERS, INC.
135 Katonah Avenue
Katonah, New York 10536

PRINTED IN THE UNITED STATES OF AMERICA
Book Design by Kenneth Hawkey

To all of the student storytellers
who have taught us so much

Contents

Preface

When we began telling stories in schools in the early 1980s we were sometimes greeted at the door by a helpful administrator who would tell us where we could pull up our car to unload the props. When we explained that we didn't use props the administrator would direct us to a room where we could change into our costumes. When we informed the administrator that we didn't wear costumes we could see a very nervous look creep onto his or her face. And we knew what the administrator was thinking: "These two people think they're going to stand up in front of two hundred kids and keep them quiet for forty-five minutes just by talking?"

We understood the administrator's nervousness, for initially we had had similar doubts. Although we had both been reintroduced to storytelling (the process of telling a story orally without a book) as adults, and had experienced first hand the power that stories had over us as listeners, it was still terrifying to be in the role of the teller. The first few times we watched a throng of noisy, unfocused children parade into an auditorium we worried that this time storytelling's magic might not work, that pandemonium would break loose. But time after time our fears were relieved as we watched our listeners become bound up in the web of a story.

When we told a participatory story the children would join in with only the slightest encouragement from us. A humorous tale found our listeners beside themselves with laughter. And when we told a quieter, more poignant tale a hush would descend over a group of kids who normally "couldn't sit still for a minute." It was as if our listeners were suspended in time, barely breathing, hanging on our every word. It is for these moments that we continue to tell stories.

Eventually, we began to tell for middle and high school students as well, and we wondered how our stories could possibly take their minds from *their* adolescent concerns. We were very careful to choose stories with which we thought they'd identify. Again, the same stillness would settle over the audience.

We had always known that stories were powerful, but we began to understand the magnitude of their power as we experienced these tellings. Stories tap deep into the unconscious of listeners and hold them in a powerful grip. As storytellers, we have the ability to make the here and now disappear for our listeners, and take them on journeys full of wonder and enchantment. Native Americans have always been acutely aware of the power of stories. Many tribes forbid the telling of stories during the growing season, fearing that plants and animals will stop their vital activities and listen to stories instead.

The storytelling renaissance in this country continues to grow. There is now much more awareness of the power of storytelling and its ability to grab and hold children's attention. Stories are usually told in schools by invited performers, and used purely as "entertainment." We have written this book because we feel strongly that storytelling is a valuable educational tool that can be an intricate, everyday part of the classroom. Teachers *and students* should be telling stories, not just invited guests.

FINDING *YOUR* WAY TO TEACH STORYTELLING

This book is about how to teach children to tell stories and how to include storytelling—both by you and by your students—as an integral part of your curriculum. It has grown out of our experiences while teaching storytelling and telling stories. We make our living as professional storytellers, and have been storytellers-in-residence at many schools where we have taught children how to be better storytellers. We have designed a "Six-week Storytelling Unit" (this is only a suggested period of time; you can shorten or lengthen it to your liking), in which students choose, learn, and tell a story. The unit was designed with grades two through eight in mind. However, we have successfully completed numerous residencies at the high school level using many of the exercises just as they are described in this book and slightly adapting others. Additionally, many of the exercises in the unit will stand alone and can be used with younger children, even preschoolers.

For those of you who need to be convinced of the value of storytelling in the classroom (or for those who are already convinced but would like to have some research and/or statistics with which to convince others), we've included "Storytelling as an Educational Tool" as Chapter 1. Since we wanted to assure you that *you* can teach your students to tell stories without a professional storyteller-in-residence, we collected the ideas and comments of teachers and librarians who have completed this task. Some are people we know or with whom we've worked; others we had either read about or heard of through the grapevine. Many students who have told stories wrote letters or filled out our questionnaires; and we've included excerpts from them as well. If you do have a professional storyteller coming into your classroom to lead a residency, the book will be a valuable resource for preparation and for follow-up activities.

Because we know from experience that the most difficult part of the unit is finding stories that are simple and short enough for students to tell, we've included twenty-five stories in Appendix B. Additionally, we've compiled an extensive bibliography of stories which are appropriate for telling (divided into two groups: grades 2–5 and 6–12) in Appendix A.

Our objective in writing this book is to suggest a way of teaching storytelling that has worked for us, and to add other perspectives as well. You will find numerous exercises that will help you teach the storytelling unit. We don't use all of them in the course of a single residency and certainly don't expect you to do so. Some of the exercises are highly recommended (they're marked with an asterisk), but you can pick and choose among the others since you are the best judge of your class' strengths and weaknesses. We hope this book will provide you with the inspiration to find *your* way of teaching storytelling.

—M. H. and M. W.

ACKNOWLEDGMENTS

Children Tell Stories: A Teaching Guide was written as a result of a three-year residency at Enfield School in Ithaca, New York, funded by the Arts in Education Program of the New York State Council on the Arts and the Ithaca City School District. The success of the project resulted in the funding being extended to include all eight Ithaca elementary schools.

We send heartfelt thanks to Nicholas Dalfino, John Efroymson, Judy Gordon, Robin Marantz Henig, Marty Kaminsky, Jeannine Laverty, June Locke, Nancy Schimmel, Ann Wasiewicz, Nancy Weiss, and Jack Williams for their time, patience, and many suggestions—all of which have made this book better. We are grateful to Sally Anne Babcock, Betty Bullock, Gay Colina, Heather Forest, Harlynne Geisler, Sharon Gibson, Mary Jane Gohl, Lois Foight Hodges, Kaye Lindauer, Mary-Eileen McClear, Joan Moore, Michael Parent, Marni Schwartz, Fran Stallings, Joyce Westgate, and Sylvia Wood for their invaluable contributions; the Reference Departments of Olin and Mann Libraries at Cornell University and the Tompkins County Public Library staff for their willingness to help us answer any of the strange questions we asked; Dede Hatch for her unobtrusive manner with a camera, and the resulting terrific photographs; Peter Carroll, for the back cover photograph and his many suggestions and insights; the third-grade teachers in the Ithaca City Schools who allowed us to come into their classrooms and take pictures at a moment's notice; Glynn Chesnut, our wonderful secretary, for typing; Jenna Headley, Colleen Hutchings, Kim Krywe, and Amie Pascuzzo for permission to print their family stories; and Tara Brown and Anna Lee Dunn for their great drawings. A special thanks to Richard Owen, whose guidance and long phone conversations were an absolute delight; our editor, Louise Waller, for her incredible eye for detail; and all the staff at Richard C. Owen Publishers for their enthusiasm about the project.

A Note on Pronouns

As storytellers, we are very aware of the power of language. When girls hear "he" or "his" all the time they may feel excluded. However, we also appreciate the beauty of language and do not want to spoil it by using the awkward he/she or him/her. Our solution to this problem has been to use plurals and alternate the use of he and she, him and her, and so on as much as possible throughout this book.

Chapter 1

Storytelling as an Educational Tool

Storytelling is the oldest form of education. Cultures throughout the world have always told tales as a way of passing down their beliefs, traditions, and history to future generations. Stories capture the imagination, engaging the emotions and opening the minds of listeners. Consequently, any point that is made in a story or any teaching that is done afterward is likely to be much more effective. Sixth grade teacher Sharon Gibson says:

> Many teachers think that storytelling will take out of class time, but it doesn't. It is part of your lesson, and makes the actual lesson much more powerful. By about the third time that I start my sixth grade class by saying "I'm going to tell you a story," they'll settle down and listen—and I've got them for the whole period. I don't have to fight for their attention. I've got it. Even when I get to the academic part I don't lose them. And their retention of the stories is amazing. Even not particularly dedicated students will remember those stories and at the end of the year they are still referring to them.

Every great teacher through the ages has used stories as a teaching tool. Why? Frank Smith, who has done research and has written extensively on the subject of literacy, notes that:

> . . . the human brain is essentially a narrative device. It runs on stories. The knowledge that we store in the brain, in our "theory of the world," is largely in the form of stories. Stories are far more easily remembered and recalled than sequences of unrelated "facts." The most trivial small episodes and vignettes are intrinsically more interesting than "data"—(*Smith, 1988, p. 178*).

Other educators agree that "storying," or the process of constructing stories in the mind, is one of the most fundamental ways of making meaning, and thus pervades all aspects of learning. The rewards of taking time to tell a story are many, and will make the extra effort worthwhile. Research backs up the idea that "even students with low motivation and weak academic skills are more likely to listen, read, write, and work hard in the context of storytelling" (*U.S. Department of Education, 1986, p. 23*).

Gordon Wells, director of the Bristol study "Language at Home and at School," notes it is generally accepted that young children find it easier to assimilate new ideas when they are presented in the form of a story. However, he believes that:

> . . . even older students find that illustrative anecdotes make general principles easier to grasp and, given the opportunity, will frequently look for such anecdotal examples in their own experience . . . As students of all ages encounter new ideas, therefore, it is helpful to illustrate these ideas with stories—with particular contextualized examples—and to support their inner storying by encouraging them to work through the story mode themselves on the way to the expression of a more abstract formulation . . . Stories provide a major route to understanding—(*Wells, 1986, p. 206*).

Kieran Egan, author of *Teaching as Storytelling: An Alternative Approach to Teaching and Curriculum in Elementary School*, believes that lessons and/or entire units can be shaped according to the engaging power of the story form. He provides a model which illustrates how to integrate imagination into the curriculum when planning classes in social studies, language arts, mathematics, and science:

> Thinking of teaching as storytelling . . . encourages us to think of the curriculum as a collection of the great stories of our culture. If we begin to think in these terms, instead of seeing the curriculum as a huge mass of material to be conveyed to students, we can begin to think of teachers in our society as connected with an ancient and honored role. Teachers are the tellers of our culture's tales—(*Egan, 1989, p. 459*).

Above all else stories are perhaps the best presents teachers can give their students, for they are beyond the power of money to buy or the world to take away. Lewis Carroll described stories as "love gifts." The stories are students' forever—from the first hearing. As far as we are concerned, there need be no other reason for sharing stories in the classroom. But the educational benefits are many and they are outlined in the rest of this chapter, where we will discuss:

How children benefit from hearing stories;

The specific benefits of folk and fairy tales, myths, and legends;

Storytelling versus story reading;

How children benefit from telling stories;

Teacher as storyteller.

HOW CHILDREN BENEFIT FROM HEARING STORIES

Numerous studies have documented the educational benefits of children listening to stories.[1] There are distinct advantages, which will be elaborated upon later, to hearing stories told without a book. These are the benefits derived from hearing stories either told or simply read aloud:

1. *Hearing stories stimulates the imagination.* Scientist Albert Einstein once said that "imagination is more important than knowledge." Yet too often this essential part of education is ignored at home and in school. In fact, in our society it is difficult for children even to trust the validity of their imaginations. Everywhere they look they are bombarded with the images of others—on television, at the movies, even in picture books. For example, many of them never heard the story of Snow White before seeing Walt Disney's movie, and thus never had a chance to form their own images. It's difficult to shake a movie image once it has been seen. Even if children hear the story again and again afterward Snow White will most likely exist forever in their minds as a Disney character.

    The immense power that the visual media wields over children's imaginations has been made clear to us by an imagery exercise that we often lead during workshops. We take one character from a story we've just told and ask children to describe him or her.[2] There is always a great variety of descriptions. After pointing out how different the descriptions are, we ask: "Now how would this experience have been different if you had all seen a movie of this story?" Initially, we assumed that they would answer: "We would all have seen him or her the same." Much to our dismay, we've found that the answer is often: "We would have seen the character the way he or she really is." Or "the way the character is supposed to be." Children need to have ample opportunity to exercise their imaginations so they can begin to see that the pictures in their minds are real too.

    Teachers can help develop children's imaginations by telling stories or reading books without pictures as well as using picture books. When only picture books are used, there is the danger that children may become dependent on pictures. We once told a class of fifth graders our version of the folk tale "Lazy Jack." Afterward, when we led the imagery exercise using the character of Jack, one student said

---

[1] *See* Gordon Wells. "Pre-school Literacy-related Activities and Success in School" in D.R. Olson *et al.,* eds. *Literacy, Language and Learning.* (Cambridge, England: Cambridge University Press, 1985); and W.H. Teale. "Reading to Young Children: Its Significance for Literacy Development" in H. Goelman *et al.,* eds. *Awakening to Literacy* (Portsmouth, N.H.: Heinemann, 1984).

[2] For a full description of the exercise *see* "The Mind's Eye," pp. 37–38.

Beauty & the Beast tell stories for a group of primary-school children.

that Jack dressed "just like Robin Hood." In fact, he insisted that everyone else's description of Jack was wrong because he had seen how Jack
looked in a book!

Picture books are wonderful, but parents and teachers should be
mindful of the fact that children eventually will move on to read books
without illustrations. Jim Trelease, in *The Read-Aloud Handbook,* relates the story of a sixth grade teacher who, when reading aloud to her
class, was chided by a student for not showing the class the pictures.
When she responded that there were no pictures the student frowned
and asked: "Then how are we supposed to know what the people look
like in the story?" (*Trelease, 1982, p. 11*).

2. *Hearing stories instills love of language in children and motivates
them to read.* In the numerous studies that have been done in the last
twenty-five years on children who learn to read early, the factor which
was most often cited as an element in reading success was that early
readers had been read to on a regular basis (*Trelease, 1982, p. 34*). In
fact, if you cease reading to children once they have learned to read,
you are in a sense punishing them for learning to read. Children need

stories read and told to them *after* they learn to read, since their listening comprehension is always far better than their reading comprehension. By reading aloud books that are at a level beyond which they can now read, you are giving them a taste of the world of reading which lies before them, and encouraging them to become better readers.

You are also reminding them of the joy of language, of how much fun it is to have the words roll off their tongues. We tell a story called *Beats Me, Claude,* which is about a man who "hankers" for a piece of apple pie such as his Mama used to make, "all bubbly, and spicy, and oozin' out of the crust" (*Nixon, 1986, p. 2*). Very early in the story children will start repeating those words with us—they especially love to say "oozin." Hearing a story is pure pleasure for them, since they can forget about the mechanics of reading and just enjoy language. Additionally, if adults look as if they're enjoying themselves while telling or reading a story, children are more likely to be drawn to books. Contrary to prevailing opinion this does *not* end with elementary school. Martha remembers that as a senior in high school her English teacher read aloud the first three or four pages of Franz Kafka's *The Metamorphosis,* a novella that begins:

> As Gregor Samsa awoke one morning from uneasy dreams he found himself transformed in his bed into a gigantic insect. He was lying on his hard, as it were armor-plated, back and when he lifted his head a little he could see his dome-like brown belly divided into stiff arched segments on top of which the bed quilt could hardly keep in position and was about to slide off completely. His numerous legs, which were pitifully thin compared to the rest of his bulk, waved helplessly before his eyes—(*Kafka, 1936, p. 1*).

Martha imagined a giant cockroach, and wondered, "Has this *really* happened to him? Is this a dream?" She checked the book out of the library after school and went home and devoured the rest of it. This technique of reading aloud part of a story, or of reading one book which is part of a series, is an effective way to encourage reading at any age.

3. *Hearing stories improves listening skills.* When stories are told or read aloud there are no visual aids, so the child's understanding of the story must be aural. This experience is very beneficial for children, since most of them watch a great deal of television where the emphasis is on the visual. Storytelling develops their concentration. The pure pleasure which children experience when listening to a story helps them to associate listening with enjoyment. As one teacher observed after taking her class to hear nationally known storyteller Jackie Torrence: "Joey has never been known to sit still for more than five minutes. On the bus he

was all over the place. I thought, this is going to be a disaster. But once the stories started he never moved, just sat there with his mouth open for a whole hour" *(Reed, 1987, p. 38)*.

4. *Hearing stories improves many language skills, such as vocabulary, comprehension, sequencing, and story recall.* An extensive study was undertaken by Dorothy H. Cohen in Harlem schools to investigate the correlation between reading aloud to students and their vocabulary skills and reading comprehension. In twenty second grade experimental classrooms teachers were required to read aloud for at least twenty minutes a day for an entire school year. The teachers in the control group continued their normal classroom procedures, using stories as an occasional treat, if they read aloud at all. At the end of the year all the students were tested and the results compared. The experimental group showed significant increases in word knowledge, quality of vocabulary, and reading comprehension. After studying the test scores Cohen concluded:

> Continued and regular listening to story books chosen for their emotional appeal and ease of conceptualization seems to aid facility in listening, attention span, narrative sense, recall of stretches of verbalization, and the recognition of newly learned words as they appear in other contexts—*(Cohen, 1968, p. 217)*.

Listening to stories familiarizes children with the characteristic rhythms and structures of language and story. It also helps them accumulate background knowledge that will aid them in interpreting what they read. Teachers have an obligation to provide children with rich and meaningful language experiences. Reports on assessment of the state of education continually point to the importance of language skills.[3] Children who lack language facility will most likely face failure in school, and possibly in life.

5. *Hearing stories encourages creative writing.* Stories beget stories. Not only will children who have heard stories told be inspired to tell and write their own stories but they will also be more likely to write stories with standard story components: beginning and end, plot, characters, setting, and theme. In other words their stories will have shape and form. After a twelve-week storytelling project one teacher commented:

> I began to notice real changes—more enthusiasm for creative writing, children getting excited about their ideas and wanting to

[3] *See* John I. Goodlad. *A Place Called School.* (N.Y.: McGraw-Hill, 1984); and U.S. National Commission on Excellence in Education. *A Nation at Risk: The Imperative for Educational Reform.* (Washington, D.C.: National Commission on Excellence in Education, 1983).

write them down and share them. I was so pleased to find children beginning to get a sense of what story is, how to set it up, and especially, how to end it. All year I'd been teaching these things, but I truly think it was the storytelling that made it real for them— (*Reed, 1987, p. 39*).

6. *When students listen to stories as a group they pick up on the many catchwords and phrases that are found in the tales. These references become the basis for a classroom subculture.* Just as stories are part of the "glue" which holds groups such as families together (for example, every family has stories such as how their ancestors came to this country or how their grandparents lost their fortune in the Great Depression) you will find that stories will create a stronger bond in your classroom as well.

> I often use the teaching tales of world cultures to make gentle points. For example, sometimes I begin the school year in my sixth grade class by telling the Chinese/African story where all guests were asked to bring wine to fill a huge vessel for a feast.[4] Instead, each secretly pours water, thinking this will not be detected if the others pour wine. After telling the story I can remind a student that I expect a more thoughtful answer by saying, "Don't bring me water." Students also enjoy the Burmese tale "A Drop of Honey"[5] in which one spilled drop, ignored as trivial, leads to the downfall of proud rulers. Later, if I have to deal with an interruption, I say, "Excuse me while I take care of this drop of honey." I've been delighted to hear students using terms and phrases from the stories with each other—(*Gibson*).

THE SPECIFIC BENEFITS OF FOLK AND FAIRY TALES, MYTHS, AND LEGENDS

1. *Folk and fairy stories teach lessons without didacticism, and stimulate emotional development.* These stories, which have been refined in their retellings through the centuries, convey at the same time overt and covert meanings, and thus tap deep unconscious feelings and desires in a child (*Bettelheim, 1977, p. 5*). Children identify with characters who struggle to overcome difficulty, and in the process they are provided with numerous problem-solving and decision-making exercises. According to child psychologist Bruno Bettelheim:

[4] Versions of this story can be found in Harold Courlander. *The King's Drum and Other African Stories.* (N.Y.: Harcourt Brace, 1962), pp. 56–57 and in Carol Kendall. *Sweet and Sour Tales from China* (N.Y.: Seabury, 1978), pp. 18–20.
[5] A version of this story can be found in Eleanor Brockett. *Burmese and Thai Fairy Tales* (Chicago: Follett, 1967), pp. 150–152.

[the child] needs—and this hardly requires emphasis at this moment in our history—a moral education which subtly, and by implication only, conveys to him the advantages of moral behavior, not through abstract ethical concepts but through that which seems tangibly right and therefore meaningful to him. The child finds this kind of meaning through fairy tales . . . More can be learned from them about the inner problems of human beings, and of the right solutions to their predicaments in any society, than from any other type of story within a child's comprehension— (*Bettelheim, 1977, p. 5*).

The late Joseph Campbell, the world's foremost authority on mythology, felt that many of the ills in our modern world are caused by the absence of a powerful mythology. When asked in an interview where street kids growing up today get their myths and rituals, he replied:

They make them up themselves. This is why we have graffiti [and violence] all over the city. These kids have their own gangs and their own initiations and their own morality, and they're doing the best they can. But they're dangerous because their own laws are not the laws of the city—(*Campbell, 1988, p. 8*).

Campbell believed that myths provide listeners with the wisdom of life, but unfortunately, "What we're learning in our schools is not the wisdom of life. We're learning technologies, we're getting information" (*Campbell, 1988, p. 9*).

By providing students with a chance not only to listen but to tell folk and fairy stories, we are fostering the development of their inner resources and providing them with messages which may help them deal with problems in their lives. Middle school teacher Marni Schwartz observed:

When I think of what I've learned about kids from watching them tell stories, Rob always comes to mind. I'd had his older brother a few years back. Their dad, a teacher himself, was somewhat critical of both boys but especially of Rob, always measuring his successes against his older brother's. Rob's choice of story was a Russian folktale about a youngest brother recapturing the firebird which had been stolen from his father's land. He had to go through many dangers and was even undermined by his older brothers in his attempts. In the end, of course, he manages to expose his brothers and win his father's love and respect. Later, when some students chose a second tale to tell, Rob retold "The Golden Goose," a story he'd loved all his life. It, too, is an example of a youngest (simple) brother winning in the end. I was glad Rob had found a way to work through his sibling rivalry through storytelling.

Children are totally focused when caught up in the web of a story.

2. *Hearing folk and fairy stories from around the world creates an awareness and appreciation of other ethnic cultures.* We once introduced our version of the classic story of "The Enormous Turnip" to a group of primary grade children by saying: "This is a very old story from Russia." We were disturbed to hear a first grader say "Yech!" reminding us of how early prejudices are formed. Children often arrive at school with biased ideas of world cultures. If they are taught only statistics about other countries in school (for example, the amount of grain sold or the square miles of a region) these prejudgments will remain. They will learn little about the people who live in a particular area. By telling folk tales to children we can teach them to appreciate the differences in people around the world, and also make them aware of the similarities. For example, hundreds of versions of the story "Cinderella" appear in world folklore, reinforcing the fact that despite our differences, people from various countries and cultures have many of the same hopes, dreams, and fears. As storyteller George Shannon has written:

> Folklore . . . offers endless insights . . . [It] allows one to
> look inside a living culture. What is important? What is proper

behavior? Who is revered and who cast out? Folk literature is affected by the people's beliefs and those in turn are often affected
by geography . . . The Eskimo hell is very cold as opposed to the
flames of the Indo-Europeans. Storytelling is social studies—a
living sharing of cultures that far outdistances the regurgitation
of statistics. Facts and figures are forgotten, but the experience of
travel be it physical or by way of storytelling is not. It remains and
grows—(*Shannon, 1979, p. 51*).

Most of us will never have the chance to travel around the world,
but one needs only a good collection of folk tales to begin the journey.
A perceptive fifth grader once said to us after we'd told a Haitian
story: "Haiti is an evil place. I know this because my Dad told me he
was in a cab in New York City, and the cab driver was from Haiti and
he told my Dad a lot of bad things about the country. But that was a
good story you told from Haiti. Maybe the people aren't really bad."

3. *Knowledge of the "old stories" is essential since it provides children
with a frame of reference for the literature and culture which they
later encounter.* Classic fairy tales and myths are the common basis of
much of our culture, especially our literature. Yet it is no longer a
given that children have heard the classic folk and fairy tales at home.
Moreover, many of the myths and legends which were once staples in
the classroom are conspicuously absent, replaced by basal readers and
works by contemporary authors. There is a great deal of excellent contemporary literature that is being included in the classroom. Yet even
this needs to be balanced by the old tales. William F. Russell, in his
introduction to *Classic Myths to Read Aloud,* bemoans the exclusion
of old stories from the classroom:

> The loss here is not just that our children are not allowed to
> be fascinated by the stories that have fascinated children for thou-
> sands of years, but that as our children grow to depend upon news-
> papers and novels and commentators instead of basal readers for
> their links with the larger world, they will not be able to understand
> the many allusions and references that are made to mythical charac-
> ters and stories by writers and speakers who just assumed that
> knowledge of these myths was shared by all—(*Russell, 1989, p. 3*).

Russell relates an incident in which he overheard two students in
the education department of a major university puzzling over a reference to "the wooden horse of Troy" in one of their texts. Finally one
student said, "And who in the world was this guy Troy, anyway?" (*Russell, 1989, p. 3*). Clearly, any references such as "Beware of Greeks

bearing gifts," or "the face that launched a thousand ships" would have no meaning for these students. The most alarming realization for Russell was that these were the teachers of tomorrow. It seemed unlikely that ancient literature would find a place in their classrooms.

As storytellers we've been acutely aware of the fact that children don't know the classics, such as "Beauty and the Beast," the story after which we're named. This became obvious when the television show "Beauty and the Beast"[6] began to air. It was clear that many children's only frame of reference for the title was the TV show, and that they either assumed we were the TV characters Katharine and Vincent (we noticed an increase in requests for autographs and a couple of times kids asked Mitch why he wasn't wearing his costume), or they thought we had named ourselves after the television show. Although we were amused by this we were also saddened. Once again the importance of our work was confirmed.

STORYTELLING VERSUS STORY READING

We are advocates of reading aloud, and realize that because it takes time to learn a story to tell, most of the stories which teachers share must be read aloud. That's fine. The benefits noted earlier apply to reading aloud as well as to telling a story. But you will find that the benefits mentioned will be even more pronounced if you put the book away now and then and just tell the story. As storyteller/teacher Denise Nessel writes:

> When the book is put aside, children become noticeably more attentive—relaxed, yet highly focused. Storytelling teachers see this again and again, with few exceptions. Eye contact is always good when there is no text to read and no book between the teacher and the group. The teacher is more aware of communicating, and the students are more fascinated with the story that comes from the familiar yet for a moment mysterious teacher . . . Closely in tune with the students, the teacher can enhance their response to the story, inviting them to chime in or pretend, with gestures and facial expressions, to be a character. Teacher and students together bring the story to life—(*Nessel, 1985, p. 379*).

The voice and personality of the teller make a story alive and vital for listeners. Without a book storytellers are free to use gestures or movements to enhance their telling. Because listeners are also actively involved in the creation of the story, the process becomes a shared experience; bonding occurs within the group.

[6] A prime time adult-oriented modern day version set in the streets of New York City.

Moreover, there are times when storytelling will work where reading aloud won't. Storyteller Tim Jennings, who was once a classroom teacher, described his experience of teaching a group of extremely troubled ten- to sixteen-year-olds how to read. He loved to read aloud and thought that was a natural starting place. But he soon found that:

> . . . all the kids felt that being read to was demeaning—baby stuff. The non-readers actually seemed provoked to feelings of physical discomfort by the steady stream of words. They squirmed; they whispered and punched; they got loudly indignant with others for squirming, whispering and punching. I'd have to stop and intervene, the thread would get lost, and the exercise—which was all it ever was—would end miserably—(*Jennings, 1981, p. 50*).

He persevered, and one day got up courage to tell a story that he knew by heart. The kids were very taken by it; and he realized later one very important reason for this was that:

> I had told a story rather than read one. My kids hated to read aloud so much that they didn't believe it could be something anybody would really want to do. When I read aloud with an appearance of relish, they automatically assumed I was faking, a practice as despicable to them as it was familiar. But they did like to talk and joke and so could accept my enthusiasm for telling a tale that was, to me at least, genuinely worthwhile. Further, whereas written literature comprises many literary devices that require a deceptive degree of listener sophistication before they can be accepted as natural, an oral tale sets up no such stylistic barriers to understanding and enjoyment. The oldest folktale can be told in language the listeners easily grasp—(*Jennings, 1981, p. 50*).

You will find the quality of listening on the part of your students to be markedly different when you tell a story directly to them. Research indicates that listeners who willingly respond may actually be in "a light trance state" when listening to a very powerful story (*Stallings, 1988, Web, p. 6*). There is a yearning for personal contact and active participation in our high-tech society. As one second grader wrote to us: "I liked your stories much better than television. The TV never asks me to do anything."

HOW CHILDREN BENEFIT FROM TELLING STORIES

The benefits of hearing stories told aloud will be further accentuated when teachers give children the opportunity to retell stories they've heard and eventually to search for their own stories to tell. By telling stories children not only begin to develop a better understanding of themselves and their world but they also gain more of an internalized sense of story form. Comprehension improves substantially.

Educational researcher Lesley M. Morrow did a study of a group of kinder-gartners where an experimental group was asked to retell a story which had been read to them "as if they were telling it to a friend who had never heard it before" (*Morrow, 1985, p. 650*). The only prompts used were: "What comes next?" Or "Then what happened?" The control group was simply asked to draw a picture about the story. Both groups were then tested for comprehension. The results showed that the experimental group scored slightly above the control group.

Morrow hypothesized that frequent retellings with guidance might have a larger effect. She undertook a second study where the experimental group was asked to retell *eight* stories, with guidance when needed. The results were much stronger. The control group improved 9.3 percent from pretest to posttest, while the experimental group improved 27.6 percent. The experimental group outperformed the control group in such activities as discussing the sequence of events, setting, theme, plot episodes, and resolution. Morrow concludes:

> The study offers rigorous empirical data and anecdotal support for the educational value of retelling stories. When so many skills are improved through its use, storytelling cannot be thought of as a frill. Classroom story role playing and retelling stories to friends and to the teacher need to be encouraged—(*Morrow, 1985, p. 659*).

Other rewards of teaching children to tell stories are plentiful.

1. *Storytelling improves self-esteem, and builds confidence and poise when speaking before a group.* As one third grade student wrote:

In thebegining I was realy scared. But I felt so good that I had the courge to do it. It mite help me when I'm big so I won't be so shy. I mite even be abell to be infront of a big croud if I had to.

In fact, speaking in front of a group is often number one on the list when adults are asked what they fear most (*Wallechinsky and Wallace, 1977, p. 469*). We, as well as many other speakers/performers with whom we've talked, have found that being comfortable in front of a group is a feeling that comes with experience. The more children are encouraged to do oral presentations while they're young, the easier it will be for them when they're older.

Teachers are often surprised to find that the best storytellers are not necessarily the children who excel in schoolwork. Getting positive attention and recognition from other students and their teacher is an excellent esteem builder. One teacher wrote:

> Michael was a six year old blond dynamo who had been deemed not ready for first grade and was in my developmental primary class. He had not solved the mysteries of print and his writing was a mystery to all but him. When it came time for sharing writing, Michael didn't say anything. One day Michael raised his hand and proceeded to tell his story out loud. He lived in a trailer and he had discovered a hole that led to a huge cavern under the ground. He wanted to explore the cavern so he secretly collected what he would need to live underground (the other children had a lot of suggestions for him at this point). When he was prepared he went on his expedition. And so the story began, a story that continued for weeks and took the class on a wide variety of adventures that lurked behind ancient doors in the cavern. Jesse protested. He lived in the trailer park, too. There was no hole under Michael's trailer, he had looked for it and it wasn't there. Michael explained the magic nature of the hole, and I explained the magic nature of Michael's storytelling ability. Michael grew large in the eyes of the class as they thought about how he had held their interest and spurred their imagination. Michael was joined by other slowly emerging readers as the year progressed and together we learned about the elements of a good story, be it written or oral. More importantly, each member of the class had ways to contribute to our learning and heads were held high. Although I had no personal experience as a storyteller and no structure to use for teaching children about storytelling, the Michael experience convinced me of its value—(*Howard*).

In the same vein, a sixth grade teacher watched the transformation of one of her students:

> Shelley was never good at anything. "Even my mother says I'll never amount to much," she told me. That was Shelley's excuse for never trying anything new. During a storytelling unit about three-fourths of the way through the year, Shelley read and reread a collection of Brer Rabbit tales she'd had since she was little. It took every ounce of courage for her to *tell* her story to the class, but once

she found herself making the class laugh at the antics and voices of her characters, she wanted to do another and another and another. After that, she never said "I can't" the rest of the year. From now on I'm doing my storytelling unit in the fall—(*Schwartz*).

Again and again the theme of improved self-esteem appears in children's comments following a storytelling unit:

> I used to be shy. I still am, but I wasn't shy when I told my story. I didn't think the principal would really come to the program, but he did and then the next day he said "Good Morning" to me in the hall. He never knew who I was before—(*Fifth grader*).

> I never knew how much thought went into telling a story. It's hard, but it was fun. I was so nervous when I first got up to tell my story, but by the end of the week I actually enjoyed telling it. If I can do that I think I can do anything—(*Eighth grader*).

> I learned to use expression instead of being boring. The hardest part was reading all the stories to try and pick one because I'm not a good reader. But everyone said I'm a good storyteller—(*Third grader*).

> I was very excited on Friday because I wanted to do my story for all the third graders very badly. Sometimes during the week I was very nervous. But when we practiced I got less nervous. I was glad too because I didn't want to mess up. I had butterflies in my stomach. But when I told my story I felt very good about myself—(*Third grader*).

> I was very nervous at the beginning and I didn't want to tell my story. But then I got excited because my friends had to do the same thing. It was so fun to hear all the stories. Well, in the end I felt very proud of myself, and I didn't want to stop telling my story. I would like to learn a lot more stories—(*Third grader*).

2. *Storytelling improves expressive language skills and stimulates inventive thinking.* Harold Rosen in his article, "The Importance of Story," emphasizes how so much of education is memorization:

> . . . mere reproduction of the words of the text book, the blackboard, the handout, the encyclopedia, the dictionary, the crammers' guides . . . there are millions of notebooks and examination papers crammed with words which are in essence transcriptions . . . But all that is quite different from retelling, from the ways in which we at one and the same time repeat the words and stories of

> others and also transform them. We elaborate, compress, innovate, and discard, take shocking liberties, delicately shift nuances . . . the whole curriculum might, could, should have as its simple quintessential rubric retelling in one's own words and the replacing of authoritative discourse with internally persuasive discourse— *(Rosen, 1986, p. 235)*.

If children are encouraged to choose a folk story and, in keeping with the oral tradition, make it their own in the retelling, they learn to be creative and to think on their feet. This creativity will inevitably carry over into other work. Children will also learn that they have a unique sensibility and method of presentation, and that no two people will ever tell a story in the same way.

3. *Storytelling improves class cooperation.* One of the recurring themes in the correspondence we receive from teachers and storytellers is their pleasure in seeing a classroom of children working closely together during a storytelling unit. It is a dynamic that continues long after the unit is over:

> In one fourth grade class where I was storyteller-in-residence the teacher was deeply concerned about the low self-esteem, back-biting and jealously among students in her classroom. She was amazed to see how eagerly the students supported and coached one another in storytelling activities. It was as if their love of the story and excitement about presenting it called a truce on infighting— *(Stallings)*.

> Although storytelling is a challenging activity, the rewards are great. It is wonderful to watch an individual's self-esteem develop and increase with the successful completion of this difficult task. The group's concern for and support of each storyteller often becomes the basis for a close class relationship— *(Babcock)*.

> Storytelling as a class activity is a great community-builder. It is a non-competitive activity in which the kids' support for each other is essential. We always stress the importance of their helping one another—*(Locke)*.

> Although my students are generally supportive of one another, I found that during my storytelling project there was an especially strong group pride in the more successful tellers in the class. Visitors to the room were often entertained by our best storytellers at the request of others in the group—*(Moore)*.

4. *Choosing, learning, and telling a story is a process in which students are learning every step of the way.* Some additional ways in which children will learn are:

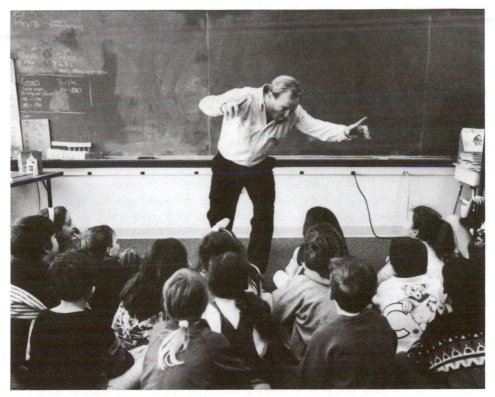

Teacher Steve Ryan tells "The Three Billy Goats Gruff" to his third-grade class at Cayuga Heights School, Ithaca, New York.

a. While choosing a story they develop an awareness of literature and a familiarity with many stories. They learn how to read with a specific purpose in mind and how to make judgments about stories. During the process of choosing a story they are also learning library and decision-making skills.

b. Children begin to understand the difference between storytelling/reading and visual media.

c. They learn what it means to be a respectful listener, and how to give constructive criticism.

d. They learn techniques for gaining and holding an audience's attention during an oral presentation (eye contact, use of voice, gestures, etc.).

e. They experience personal growth through risk taking.

f. Through this hands-on experience children learn to appreciate the hard work that goes into any art form and thus they gain a greater understanding of all the arts.

Inevitably, some children are very good storytellers while others are not. What's important is not the final product but the process. Whether students tell a story well or not they will most assuredly have learned a great deal. Many will learn in ways you never imagined, as storyteller Michael Parent observed:

> I was teaching high-school English. Clarence, my favorite "reluctant learner" and class comedian, badly needed to make up lost credit to pass Junior English. He was given a number of options. He chose to do dramatic readings of Aesop's Fables, starting with "The Boy Who Cried Wolf." He worked hard, did very well and the positive response seemed to boost him into more involvement with other assignments. He did pass the course, and did become a senior. It was in his senior year that a fellow teacher told me of another development that could well have been an outgrowth of the "readings." Clarence had begun to illustrate his point of view in this teacher's class discussions with riveting stories about such non-comedic subjects as the sufferings of his slave ancestors. He was still a funny guy, but he was now being paid attention to even when he chose to be serious. The story reading and telling seemed to have carried him across that thin line between class clown and class philosopher.

5. *You will learn a great deal from listening to your students tell stories.* Through storytelling teachers may discover more about how students learn. One teacher described a student so shy and withdrawn, so unable to function in class that . . .

> I had written her off as severely learning disabled . . . [However], Patty showed a complete metamorphosis at storytelling time, became confident, animated, eager to act out and retell the story. I came to see that Patty's auditory skills are her strength. I am now reevaluating the results of a battery of tests. Without the storytelling project she might never have had this chance—(*Reed, 1987, p. 39*).

You will be amazed and inspired by your students' courage, creativity, and lively imaginations. Some will begin to improvise, fabricate, and ad-lib far beyond what you could ever teach them, as one teacher commented:

> Ellen was a born storyteller. I didn't teach her anything; I just gave her the kind of environment where her talent could blossom.

I can still see her doing Sendak's *Chicken Soup with Rice* in my middle school class. She had her pseudo-sophisticated peers giggling their way through the seasons "siiiiiiipping once, siiiiiiipping twice . . . "

A small group of tellers gave an evening performance for parents and community members at our local library. Ellen had chosen to be the last teller of the evening. The audience was saturated with stories and tended to talk between each one. Ellen walked out and stood with her back to the audience until the crowd hushed. She was twelve at the time. I thought, "Who taught her that?" Somehow she just instinctively knew she had to grab her weary listeners. Finally, she whirled around and burst into the story. "Mr. Possum once had a beeeeauuuutiful loooooong tail." Dramatically she reached to brush her tail. Not one of us was too tired for another story.

Ellen's sixteen now and storytelling for her summer camp jobs and for story-hours at the local library. I asked her to present a workshop with me for middle school teachers. She told them, "In storytelling, you can be anyone you ever wanted to be. You can see what it feels like to be a wicked witch, a conceited schoolgirl, a Russian peasant who's emigrated to America. And sometimes it's good to get away from who you really are for a little while. That's what I like about storytelling"—(*Schwartz*).

TEACHER AS STORYTELLER

Many teachers, although enthusiastic about the idea of their students telling stories, are reticent to try it themselves.

I wanted to teach my third graders to tell stories but I was terrified because I realized I'd have to tell a story myself. It reminded me of a time when I took one of my classes roller skating even though I'd never skated in my life. A lot of my kids hadn't either, so I decided I'd have to try it. My ineptitude on the rink put me in touch with the feelings of frustration that kids encounter all the time as they try to learn new things. I have been a better teacher ever since. When I worked alongside my kids at telling my first story, it made me very aware of the difficulties they were confronting. I managed to work through my fear along with them, and was astonished to see how fantastic some of my kids were. We had a great time!—(*Kaminsky*).

You don't have to be an expert teller in order to get students telling stories. You can begin by arranging for professional storytellers to visit your school and by showing videotapes of a variety of storytellers. But it will be an inspiration to students if you choose a story to tell and take part in the exercises that we suggest. As one third grade teacher noted:

As the teacher, you must be a model for your students. We had a visiting storyteller who got the students excited about telling stories, but it wasn't until I told my first story that student enthusiasm for storytelling really started to grow. As my students began to tell stories, I saw numerous positive changes in the class. I witnessed a non-reader blossom into a self-confident, enthusiastic learner. He now wants to be a professional storyteller and continues to learn and tell stories to the class. The most often asked question in my room now is: "Can I tell a story to the class?"—(*Gohl*).

For those of you who are hesitant about telling stories yourself, start slowly. Begin by using anecdotes from your life as an easy source for stories. This approach adds informality to the telling and eliminates extensive learning time. If you enjoy that, make a commitment to learn a short folk tale. Undoubtedly, many of you already know a number of stories virtually by heart from having read them so many times. Try telling one of those without the book, or consider turning to the story "The Tailor" at the beginning of Chapter 6. It's a good choice for a beginning story because it's short, simple, and universal. We have told the story and done the exercise which follows it with first graders to middle/high school students to adults.

Although this book is meant primarily as a guide for teaching students to tell stories, teachers will learn a great deal about how to tell stories themselves. If you want to read more, we've included a bibliography of some of the best books on storytelling in Appendix A. Two excellent sources of stories for beginners are *Twenty Tellable Tales* and *When the Lights Go Out: Twenty Scary Tales to Tell* both by Margaret Read MacDonald. We've included a list of our favorite story sources in the appendix under the title "Sources of Stories for Teachers to Tell or Read Aloud." "Suggested Stories for Students to Tell" is also in the Appendix. (If *they* can tell them, *you* can certainly tell them.)

Once you take the leap and tell your first story it will be much easier the next time. The initial telling is always the most difficult. Martha procrastinated for a year before telling her first story. Part of the problem was that she had chosen as her first story Margery Williams' *The Velveteen Rabbit,* a long picture book that would probably take twenty minutes or more to tell. Once she finally gave up that idea and chose a short folk tale she learned it in a couple of days. It is best not to choose a long story or a literary story until you've developed confidence as a storyteller. Pick a short, simple folk tale that you love and that you think will interest your students. Practically speaking, the small amount of time that the busy teacher can allot to preparation will most likely mean that your telling will be less than polished. Remember, as a sixth grade teacher reflected, "You don't have to tell a story perfectly to be successful. Children love the stories and are very forgiving audiences" (*Gibson*).

If some of your colleagues are interested in storytelling you'll be able to tell stories to their classes and vice-versa. That way you'll be able to work on refining your story by telling it to a variety of audiences, and all of your students will have the benefit of hearing many different stories and storytellers.

We recently told stories in a rural school which included students from kindergarten through twelfth grade. Several students and teachers mentioned a high school teacher who came every year to tell stories to the lower grades. We eventually found that his repertoire consisted of two good scary stories, yet he was already a legend in the school.

We encourage you to learn a story. It will open a world of delights for you and your students.

Chapter 2

Introducing Children to the Idea of Telling Stories

Some of these ideas can be used in a classroom to make students aware that everyone is a storyteller, and to get them used to the idea of giving oral presentations for the rest of the class. Any of the three activities described below can be used with children as young as kindergarten level, and will stand alone if you choose not to do the six-week storytelling unit. They could also be used as an introduction to the unit. For example, if you planned to utilize the storytelling unit in January/February, you could use some of these activities throughout the fall.

FAMILY/EXPERIENCE STORIES

Storytelling is a natural part of our lives, something we all do whether we realize it or not. We all have family or experience stories—tales of eccentric relatives, of what we remember from our first day of school, or the best present we ever received or gave; or perhaps stories of a time when we were lost, or very embarrassed, or very scared, or when we laughed so hard we cried. To begin to investigate the storyteller inside each of us, try storyteller Harlynne Geisler's suggestion of starting with a game:

> I teach storytelling to students in 4th through 9th grade. This year I've been starting right off with a game I learned from Doug Lipman.[7] I tell the class two stories that both supposedly happened to me as a child. They have to vote on whether each of the stories is true or a fib. Then each of them gets a chance to "stump the class" by standing up and telling about something that happened to them or by telling a fib. This game approach excites and interests them. After playing it, I explain that we all have many

[7] For other game suggestions *see* Doug Lipman. "Story Games." *The National Storytelling Journal* Part 1: 3.4(1986):24–26; Part 2: 4.1(1987):12–17.

stories that we already know—all the incidents that have happened in our lives—or that we can make up (the fibs) and that we are all already story-tellers. Most of them have never thought of themselves as storytellers with many tales under their belts. Knowing that, the idea of learning more about storytelling doesn't seem so scary, even to the shy children—(*Geisler*).

Family and experience stories are rich sources of material both for telling stories and for creative writing. For other ideas *see* Chapter 9, "Helping Children to Develop Family and/or Experience Stories for Telling."

TELLING JOKES OR RECITING POEMS

Most children can relate to the idea of telling a joke. Jokes are really nothing more than very short stories. Similarly, reciting a short poem is something that many children enjoy. Having each student choose a joke, riddle, poem, or even a tongue-twister to present to the class is a good introduction to telling a story. It gets them up in front of the class for a brief time, and prepares them for many facets of the storytelling unit, such as the importance of eye contact, timing, practicing, and being prepared.

Jokes can be an especially good introduction because they are not usually repeated word-for-word, although children may fall into this habit if they are learning the jokes out of a book rather than learning them from friends. Unlike jokes and stories, poems do require strict memorization. The difference can be made clear when you move on to the storytelling unit by using the various exercises we suggest for showing how stories change.

The more chances your students have to practice their oral presentations, the more comfortable they will become in front of others. Try sending small groups of students to other classrooms to tell their poems and jokes. You could, for example, divide your class into groups of four or five, let them pick a theme such as "Spooky Poems," and come up with a program that they could "take on the road."

Here are a few suggested sources:

Adoff, Arnold, ed. *My Black Me: A Beginning Book of Black Poetry.* N.Y.: Dutton, 1974 (ages 10 and up).

Bodecker, N.M. *A Person from Britain Whose Head Was the Shape of a Mitten and Other Limericks.* N.Y.: Atheneum, 1980.

Cole, Joanna. *The Laugh Book.* Garden City, N.Y.: Doubleday, 1986.

_____, ed. *A New Treasury of Children's Poetry: Old Favorites and New Discoveries.* N.Y.: Doubleday, 1984.

de Regniers, Beatrice Schenk, ed. *Sing a Song of Popcorn*. N.Y.: Scholastic, 1988.

Kohl, Marguerite, and Frederica Young. *Jokes for Children*. N.Y.: Hill and Wang, 1963.

Lobel, Arnold, ed. *The Random House Book of Mother Goose*. N.Y.: Random House, 1986.

_____. *Whiskers and Rhymes*. N.Y.: Greenwillow, 1985.

Prelutsky, Jack. *New Kid on the Block*. N.Y.: Greenwillow, 1984.

_____. *Tyrannosaurus Was a Beast*. N.Y.: Greenwillow, 1988.

_____, ed. *The Random House Book of Poetry for Children*. N.Y.: Random House, 1983.

Schwartz, Alvin. *A Twister of Twists, A Tangler of Tongues*. Philadelphia: Lippincott, 1972.

Silverstein, Shel. *A Light in the Attic*. N.Y.: Harper and Row, 1981.

_____. *Where the Sidewalk Ends*. N.Y.: Harper and Row, 1974.

Smith, William Jay. *Laughing Time*. N.Y.: Delacorte, 1980.

Viorst, Judith. *If I Were in Charge of the World and Other Worries*. N.Y.: Atheneum, 1981.

Worth, Valerie. *Small Poems*. N.Y.: Farrar, Straus & Giroux, 1986.

RETELLING STORIES

As we noted earlier we feel strongly that stories should be shared often in the classroom with no other purpose than providing listeners with pleasure, a spiritual uplift, and the chance to partake of the important business of daydreaming. Because students are so receptive to stories, and since they respond to events and characters, making links with their own lives and other story experiences, stories will often naturally trigger discussions and can easily lead to related activities. It is important that the teacher should always respect children's rights to interpret the story for themselves. Bruno Bettelheim wrote:

Explaining to a child why a fairy tale is so captivating to him destroys the story's enchantment, which depends to a considerable degree on the child's not quite knowing why he is delighted by it . . . Adult interpretations, as correct as they may be, rob the child of the opportunity to feel that he, on his own, through repeated hearing and ruminating about the story, has coped successfully with a difficult situation. We grow, we find meaning in life, and security in ourselves by having understood and solved personal problems on our own, not by having them explained to us by others . . . Fairy tales enrich the child's life and give it an enchanted quality just because he does not quite know how the stories have worked their wonder on him—(*Bettelheim, 1977, pp. 18–19*).

Retelling a story is one activity that offers children the opportunity to interpret the story for themselves. It is a natural process with which we're all familiar. When children tell a friend about a movie they've seen or a story they've read, they're taking what they remember of the story/movie and relating it in their own words. Storyteller Fran Stallings has made retelling an integral part of her work in the classroom:

I firmly believe that the natural human way to learn storytelling is by oral/aural IMITATION. That's how we're programmed to learn other language skills! So I emphasize oral presentation of stories to beginners, followed by lots of retelling exercises. I use only traditional folk tales which have winnowed out everything that doesn't work orally. In a recent school residency I told a story to 24 fourth graders. We went over the basic plot line, and they practiced retelling the story first to a partner and then in small groups. Afterwards, each big kid took a cluster of younger students off under a tree and told their stories. The second graders loved it, and the fourth graders were so enthusiastic that they came in begging to tell to first graders next. Both teachers and administrators remarked that this is the most powerful esteem-builder they've seen—(*Stallings*).

Even very young children can be encouraged to retell stories, and some will grab any opportunity to do so, as Lois Foight Hodges, a librarian at the Schenectady, New York, Public Library, discovered:

Called out of a preschool group one day I came back to find a five-year-old confidently seated upon my stool, halfway through "Where the Wild Things Are" while the fourteen others gave her absorbed attention. (They don't always give *me* absorbed attention!)—(*Hodges*).

Be selective in the stories you ask your class to retell. Above all else you must be sure not to turn retelling into an assignment that will detract from children's listening pleasure. Stories that children are asked to retell should be short and simple enough for them to grasp easily. Some stories may have a magical quality that leaves listeners in an enchanted, almost dreamlike state

Fourth graders listen attentively to a classmate's story.

you wouldn't want to destroy. Others may be too long or complicated for them to tell.

We have provided an excellent story ("The Tailor," Chapter 6) for a beginning retelling exercise. Many of the short stories included in Appendix B (for example, "How the Rabbit Lost His Tail," "The Sun and the Wind," "The Dog and His Shadow," and "The Boy Who Turned Himself into a Peanut") are simple and short enough to be retold by young children, especially when you've shared the story more than once. After telling the story, review it with the children by asking, "What happened first?" Then, "What happened next?" Make a brief outline on the board. They can begin by telling the story to a partner. Small groups can tell it in round-robin fashion or with one student serving as the narrator while others take speaking roles or even mime roles. Eventually, they'll know the story well enough so that they can all tell it individually. Sylvia Wood, a second grade teacher who was fortunate to have Fran Stallings work in her classroom, shared these comments:

> Fran would tell a story and then the children would help me to outline the bare bones of the story on the blackboard. Afterwards, students

would pair up and tell the story with a partner. Eventually they told it to the class and to other classrooms. We began to use the same technique with their reading material which had a profound effect on their story comprehension skills. They were a very immature class from the start, with delayed skills in reading and writing *and* the fact that they demanded one-on-one attention, were impatient with each other, and had difficulty cooperating. The storytelling led to vastly improved interpersonal skills and enhanced self-confidence. Audiences rewarded them with huge amounts of attention, appropriately won. Perhaps more important, in the exercises they grudgingly paid attention to each other. Their oral language experience has also carried over into their writing. I have never had a class do such creative, coherent, detailed and interesting writing. Nora is writing a series of stories about Miss Skinney, an eccentric substitute teacher. She is very entertaining. It's hard to believe she's just a child. I was initially very hesitant about telling stories myself, but my students have won me over. Now I'm a storyteller, too!—(*Wood*).

Encourage children to share stories at home as well. We often tell children that their parents work hard all day long and would really appreciate it if someone tucked them into bed and told *them* a bedtime story!

Read and Retell (Brown and Cambourne, 1990) is an excellent source that describes how to use *written* retelling as a strategy for assessing children's comprehension of texts and evaluating their control over language structure and conventions. It includes thirty-eight stories. Students read the stories, put them aside, and then retell them—in writing—from memory. They then compare their versions with classmates' versions. This would be a good introduction to the idea of interpreting folk tales in children's own words. Many of the stories would also be appropriate for the *oral* retelling exercise described earlier.

For a perspective on the uses of retelling as a way of teaching writing and language skills for *older* students, read Betty Rosen's *And None of It Was Nonsense: The Power of Storytelling in School.* It is an inspiring book by a teacher who worked with a multi-language, multi-cultural group of twelve- to eighteen-year-old boys who were "not confident about their abilities." At times she would elicit oral stories from students by asking questions such as, "Were you ever scared in the middle of the night?" Or "Does anyone have a scar? How'd you get it?" More often she would tell stories, with an emphasis on Greek myths and other traditional tales, and then ask students to retell the story (in writing) either as she had told it or from a different point of view, or with as many changes as students chose to make. Rosen writes:

> To use storytelling as a major way of teaching and learning there must be, above all else, the certainty that children (all children, all people) have the capacity to transform and create out of what they receive . . . To close the books, look at the kids, tell them a story from scratch, then ask them to

tell that story back again . . . presupposes an enormous confidence in people to know that something new and good will come from every child—*(Rosen, 1988, p. 8)*.

Her students' perceptive and varied writings, many examples of which are included in her book, are powerful testimony to the fruits that such confidence can bear.

Chapter 3

Planning and Preparing for a
Six-week Storytelling Unit

DESCRIPTION

In the next few chapters we will outline a six-week storytelling unit in which students will choose, learn, and tell a story to their classmates. They will also be encouraged to share their stories in other classrooms, for community organizations, and to give an evening performance for parents and friends. We realize that your school day is already crowded with curriculum requirements and that it is hard to squeeze yet another project into your busy days. Lucy Calkins discusses this issue in *The Art of Teaching Writing:*

> . . . time is our scarcest resource. Teachers often ask me, "How do I squeeze writing in on top of everything else?" My suggestion is simple: don't. Instead of squeezing one more thing into the crowded curriculum, I suggest that we each take a good hard look at our school day to determine what is no longer needed there. My husband and I recently moved from one Connecticut town to another, and the thing that surprised me most about the move was the amount of junk we had accumulated. We took fifteen *car loads* of trash to the dump. Sometimes I think that if we, as teachers, want to move on, we too need to take car loads to the dump. Most of our curricula still include things we no longer need or no longer feel strongly about. It is only by cleaning out some old things that we can give time and space to new ones—(*Calkins, 1986, p. 24*).

Make time for the storytelling unit. The skills and self-confidence children acquire, the sense of class cooperation and spirit that are aroused, and, most importantly, the enthusiasm for learning that is generated by the unit will make every moment you spend on it worthwhile.

APPROPRIATE GRADE LEVELS

The unit we have designed is for grades two through eight. We have successfully completed this project with ninth through twelfth graders, and many of the exercises can be used just as they are with older students, while others can be slightly adapted. "Suggested Stories for Students to Tell" in Appendix A includes ideas for younger tellers as well as older ones.

MATERIALS NEEDED

When we lead workshops for teachers on developing a storytelling unit in their classrooms one of the first questions is invariably: "What do I need to get started?" The answer is quite simple: A library that includes a good selection of folk tales. As the project progresses, you will find that there are some materials that will greatly help your students, although they are by no means essential to success. Since reading a story to a blank tape can be helpful for the learning process, tape recorders and blank tapes will come in handy for those students who do not have access to them at home. In addition, if a video recorder and VCR are available they can be used for taping students while they are telling their stories and then playing tapes back so that children can evaluate their telling. The machines are also useful for showing commercial videos of professional storytellers.

PREPARATION

Although this unit can be completed successfully by classroom teachers on their own, it will be much easier if the aid of the school librarian, resource teachers, and parents are enlisted for various aspects of the project. The librarian can help develop a pool of stories from which students can choose. Depending on your style, this pool may include the entire folk-tale collection in the school library (you can also check books out of the local public library to add to the collection) or a selected group of stories. Before developing the pool, read the discussion, "The Process of Choosing" in Chapter 5. If you wish to limit students to certain stories use the Bibliography of "Suggested Stories for Students to Tell" in Appendix A. Add any stories of your choosing to the pool. To get you started, we have included twenty-five folk tales in Appendix B that are good stories for telling.

You may choose to photocopy individual stories from collections, as long as photocopying falls within the "fair use" guidelines of the U.S. Copyright Law. Otherwise, mark individual stories for reference within collections. Be

Beauty & the Beast demonstrate the use of facial expression and gestures during a classroom workshop for fifth graders.

sure to always keep the original book or copy in the classroom because, as you know, children may lose anything not attached to their bodies. It is important that students are able to take their stories home in order to practice. If photocopying is not possible, some teachers have had the children copy the story in longhand; that way they have more invested in it and aren't as likely to lose it.

Throughout the project you will want students to hear as many stories as possible, so call on anyone you know who tells stories well and would be willing to visit your class. If colleagues are interested in storytelling, try team teaching the unit, thus taking advantage of each other's strengths. If school librarians are interested in storytelling they can help out as well as lead some of the exercises.

During the course of the project you can ask other support personnel—such as reading, speech, or resource teachers—to help students who are having difficulty choosing and/or learning stories. For example, if the reading teacher is working with a nonreader, he or she can read a number of stories to the student who can then choose one of the stories to tell. Then he or she can read the story into a tape recorder so that the student can listen to it over and over again.

Marginal or nonreaders can prove to be very good storytellers when given individual attention, as we have seen. One of our fondest memories is when Jeremy, a second grader who could not read, told "The Sweet Tooth" from James Marshall's *Tons of Fun*. He had initially seemed disinterested, probably because he was embarrassed that he couldn't read in order to choose a story. A resource teacher worked with him, and once he had picked his story he knew instinctively how to tell it. In the story when the hippopotamus Martha tries to get her friend George to stop eating too many sweets he will not listen to reason. So Martha lights up a big cigar and begins to puff on it to make her point. As Jeremy described Martha turning a "peculiar color" his classmates laughed happily. For the first time in his school career Jeremy was the class star.

It would be helpful if the teacher sends a note home to parents informing them of the project and enlisting their help. Children who practice their stories at home will feel much more confident when they tell them in front of classmates. If tape recorders are available at home parents can help their children read the stories to a blank tape (*see* "Sample Letter to Parents"). If you are comfortable with the idea of having parents volunteer in your classroom encourage them to participate in the storytelling project when you send the letter home.

HANDOUT: SAMPLE LETTER TO PARENTS

Dear Parents:

During the month of February we will be doing a storytelling project in our classroom. Each student will choose a short story (under ten minutes) and tell it in front of the others in the class from memory and without the book. This should be a great opportunity for learning poise and self-confidence when speaking before a group, and will also help students improve their expressive language skills.

You can help by encouraging your child to go over the story again and again until he or she has learned it. If you have a tape recorder let your child read it to a blank tape so that he or she can listen to it whenever the opportunity arises. Let your child know you are a willing listener, and be prepared to listen to the story many times and to give *constructive* criticism. A list of basic storytelling techniques is attached.

Thanks so much for helping with what should prove to be a fun-filled project. We are planning to celebrate at the end of the project with an evening performance by those students who volunteer to tell their stories. The performance will be on March 10, 1990, at 7:00 P.M. We hope you will be able to attend.

Sincerely,

Enc: Suggestions to Help You Learn Your Story
Techniques to Keep in Mind as You Tell Your Story

SIX-WEEK STORYTELLING UNIT: SAMPLE TIMETABLE

Try to include one story as part of every session, told either by you or invited guests or professional storytellers on video or audiocassette.

	Monday	Tuesday	Wednesday	Thursday	Friday
Week 1	Storytelling performance (by professional teller, librarian, or teacher). (Letters go home to parents.)	Introductory session: Discussion on importance of telling stories. Exercise: "The Mind's Eye."	How to Choose a Story. ←——————————————— Story Selection ———————————————→ Set aside 20 minutes each day for students reading to select stories.		
Week 2	←————————————————————————————— Story Selection —————————————————————————————→				
Week 3	←————————————————————————————— How to Learn a Story —————————————————————————————→ Exercise: How a Story Changes. (Handout: How to Learn Your Stories.)	←— Discussion: How to Practice. —→ Exercise: Pictorial Outlines and/or Story Maps.	Students tell story to a partner, using outlines.	Discussion: Beginnings and Endings. Various Exercises: Improving Oral-Descriptive Skills. How to Improvise Language. [Allow 10 minutes for students to practice stories with a different partner, using outlines if necessary.]	
Week 4	←————————————————————————————— How to Tell a Story —————————————————————————————→ Discussion of use of voice, with various exercises. Students practice stories without outlines. (Handout: Techniques for Telling.)			Discussion of use of gestures, with various exercises. Allow time each day for students to practice telling their stories with partners and eventually with small groups.	
Week 5	←——————— How to Tell a story ———————→ Discussion on developing characters, with exercises.	Developing poise and presence. Exercises: Presence, eye contact.		←— Children tell stories with critiques. —→	
Week 6	Critiques. —→	←————————————————————————————— Storytelling Festival —————————————————————————————→ Children tell stories to entire class Party to celebrate.		Students who volunteer can go to other classes, senior citizens' —→ homes, or community groups to tell their stories.	Parent's night.

Chapter 4

Introducing the Storytelling Unit

OBSERVING STORYTELLERS

The best way to arouse enthusiasm for a storytelling project is to kick it off by having a storytelling program, whether by a professional storyteller, the school librarian, another teacher at your school who is a good storyteller, or you. One of the main ways storytellers acquire their skill is by observing other storytellers demonstrating their art. Throughout the project you will want to give your students as many opportunities as possible to observe different styles of storytelling. *Try to include one story (told by you or others) as part of each session.*

Be resourceful. Ask around to find good local storytellers. Consult *The National Storytelling Directory*[8] which lists professional storytellers, organizations, festivals, and conferences throughout the United States. Check the school and local public libraries for videotapes and audiotapes of storytellers. Although these can never begin to capture the full impact of a live performance they can introduce your students to a very wide range of styles and traditions of storytelling. If you expose students to a number of storytellers chances are they will be inspired by or be able to identify with at least one teller; and will certainly become very aware that there are many ways in which to tell a story (*see* "Storytelling on Video- and Audiocassette," Appendix A).

DISCUSSION OF THE IMPORTANCE OF TELLING STORIES

Lead a class brainstorming session on why people told stories in the past and why it's still important to tell them. Some of the reasons you will want to cover are these:

---

[8]To order a copy write The National Association for the Preservation and Perpetuation of Storytelling (NAPPS), P.O. Box 309, Jonesborough, TN 37659.

Weirui shares "How the Long-tailed Bear Lost His Tail" with her classmates and their parents.

1. *To stimulate the imagination* and allow listeners to create their own unique images.

2. *To entertain.* Ask students to think of other ways in which people entertained one another before the time of radio and television (for example, singing, dancing, playing games, making music, reading, talking, etc.). This is a good opportunity to remind them that they do not always have to turn on the television.

3. *To teach lessons.* Cultures have always used stories to pass down the beliefs and values of their societies. Discuss some possible reasons why classic stories, such as "Little Red Riding Hood" (or the stories they have just heard live or on tape), were originally told.

4. *To teach history.* Remind them that storytellers were once vital to the preservation of the history of early civilizations. Their stories were the records which were passed from generation to generation by word-of-mouth. With the advent of alphabets, writing implements, and eventually

the printing press, storytelling lost its special position in the community. In the twentieth century the invention and widespread exposure to television and other visual media almost caused storytelling to become a lost art.

5. *To pass on folklore.* Explain that folklore includes the traditional customs, tales, or sayings that are preserved orally among a people. Give them a familiar example such as jump-rope rhymes and other playground jingles that children preserve strictly by word-of-mouth:

> John and Jane sitting in a tree
> K-I-S-S-I-N-G.
> First comes love,
> Then comes marriage,
> Then comes Jane with a baby carriage.

6. *To explain things they didn't understand.* Every culture has "why," or *pourquoi,* stories that explain, for example, why the bear has a short tail or how the moon and stars came to be.

*EXERCISE: THE MIND'S EYE

Children in our society are used to having all the images shown to them on television and in movies. Thus it is important for them to recognize the process that goes on in their mind's eye while they listen to a story. The purpose of this exercise is to show them how storytelling and reading are different from these other media in that each listener creates his or her unique images.

After they have listened to a storyteller (whether live or on tape) ask your students: "What did you see as the storyteller told the stories?" They may simply reply: "I saw pictures in my mind of what was happening in the story." If they start to describe particular scenes, let them go on for a while and then lead them to the more general answer.

Pick a character that was particularly vivid for you in one of the stories. It is best to choose a character who was not described in too much detail. Have students close their eyes and remember how they pictured the character (in silence, so they are not influenced by others' descriptions). Asking them questions will facilitate the process. For example: "What did Jack look like? How old do you think he was? How would you describe his face? His eyes? Nose? Ears? What color was his hair? Was it straight or curly, combed or uncombed? What kind of clothes was he wearing?" Then ask a few volunteers to describe to the rest of the class how they pictured Jack. There will be many different

*We have marked the exercises we feel are essential to the unit with an asterisk. You can pick and choose among the others since you are the best judge of your class' strengths and weaknesses.

images of Jack, and you can point out that this is what makes storytelling so interesting and so much fun. All of the listeners create their own images, whereas when they watch television or a movie they all see exactly the same images. Ask students if they have ever read a book and then seen a movie of the same book. What was their reaction?

If you feel your students need more experience with imagery we suggest these books:

Bagley, Michael T., and Karin K. Hess. *200 Ways of Using Imagery in the Classroom*. N.Y.: Trillium, 1984.

de Mille, Richard. *Put Your Mother on the Ceiling: Children's Imagination Games*. N.Y.: Penguin, 1976.

Chapter 5

Helping Students Choose a Story

DISCUSSION OF TYPES OF STORIES

To give students an understanding of the different kinds of stories from which they can choose, tell/read them an example from each of the types of stories listed here. Jack Maguire gives a thorough description of types of stories, as well as an example for each type in his *Creative Storytelling: Choosing, Inventing, and Sharing Tales for Children.* Legends, fairy tales, myths, fables, and tall tales all fall under the general heading of folk tale, but have specific characteristics which make them unique.

FOLK TALE

A folk tale is a story which has been handed down through the ages from one generation to another through word-of-mouth, and thus belongs to a particular culture rather than an individual. Some of the stories may have originated as literary tales, but were told so often that they became part of the oral tradition. The characters tend to be stereotypes of ordinary people (for example, an evil old man or a wise woman), although extraordinary things do happen to them. Because folk tales are created by the people they give us many insights into the cultures from which they spring. The themes in folk tales are universal and timeless. Folk tales generally lack descriptive passages and rely almost exclusively on plot.

LEGEND

A story about people, places, or events that have some basis in historical fact is a legend. However, the stories have been retold so often and the incidents exaggerated to such a degree that it is usually impossible to prove they actually happened. Examples include tales about Robin Hood, Johnny Appleseed, John Henry, Pocahontas, and Davy Crockett.

FAIRY TALE

A fairy tale is a story that is usually the creation of a specific author. It differs from a legend in that it is almost always fictional in intent. The fairy tale is frequently set in a never-never land where all kinds of supernatural events take place. It tends to be longer, more descriptive, and more complicated than other folk tales.

MYTH

A story that attempts to explain a natural phenomenon or a specific belief or practice in a particular culture is a myth. For example, many cultures have myths that explain how the universe was created, or how people came to live on earth. Often myths have to do with religion and depict the actions of god-like beings.

FABLE

A fable is a story in which the main characters are usually animals behaving like people. It always teaches a moral, which is usually clearly stated at the end.

TALL TALE

A tall tale involves characters that are larger than life. These stories evolved out of the American frontier experience. Although they may be based, however remotely, on actual happenings it is unabashed exaggeration that gives these tales their flavor. The adventures of Paul Bunyan, Mike Fink, and Pecos Bill—to name a few—are well-documented in American folklore.

LITERARY STORY

A literary story is written by a particular author. These stories can be difficult to tell because they rely so much on the beauty and power of the language and so the teller must adhere to the text as closely as possible. *Rootabaga Stories* by Carl Sandburg and *Just So Stories* by Rudyard Kipling are examples of this kind of story.

THE PROCESS OF CHOOSING

The stories students choose are very important to their feelings of success in this project. For some students this may mean choosing a story that is no

In the folk-tale section of the library students search for a story to tell.

longer than three or four sentences. The most important quality of the story is that it be one they really love. Only if they have been moved by the story will they be able to move their listeners. The story should not be assigned, since students' enthusiasm for a story is crucial. Ken Goodman, a leading proponent of the whole-language approach to teaching, writes:

> Kids need to feel that what they are doing through language they have chosen to do because it is useful, or interesting, or fun for them. They need to own the processes they use: to feel that the activities are their own, not just school work or stuff to please the teacher. What they do ought to matter to them personally—(*Goodman, 1986, p. 31*).

We have found that few children know their own capabilities. Some children can read far beyond the level of story they can tell orally; while some poor readers are excellent storytellers. Your gentle guidance will be very helpful. It is better for a child who has difficulty learning or who is very shy to tell a five-sentence story and feel successful than to struggle with a longer, more complicated one and end up not telling it. As elementary school librarian June Locke reflected:

I used to have children find their own stories for telling. However, they would frequently choose inappropriate stories or become frustrated in their search, thereby dooming them from the start. Now they choose from a collection of about seventy-five stories, divided into levels of difficulty in a large file box. This has worked very well, insuring a successful experience for everyone—(*Locke*).

We urge you to restrict younger children and those who have never told a story to a preselected pool of stories rather than turning them loose in the library. We feel this will greatly increase the success of the project. (*See* the extensive bibliography, "Suggested Stories for Students to Tell" at the end of Appendix A.) Try to have a pool of at least fifty stories for a classroom of twenty-five students. You should, however, remain open to considering other stories that students show an interest in telling. A child may be drawn to a particular story because it fills an emotional need, as one middle-school teacher noted:

> Gautham's family emigrated to the U.S. from India. *He* was Schenectady-born, a real upstate New York American kid, sometimes to his parents' dismay. When he chose *Curious George,* I was new to storytelling and afraid a book whose joy relies so much on pictures wouldn't make a successful telling. Gautham assured me he could "make the pictures live" and he proved he could. Among other images, we "saw" George, the little monkey, climb a coconut tree in the museum because for a minute he thought he was back in Africa. Of course the tree wasn't real and George got in a lot of trouble. Later, reflecting on Gautham's choice, I thought about how his roots were in a foreign land just as George's were, yet how in America they were learning sometimes painfully to adapt. Gautham's telling, like Rey's pictures of George, stole our hearts—(*Schwartz*).

If you wish to extend the unit over a longer period of time the choosing phase is the natural place to do it. This is a chance to introduce students to a wide body of literature. Ann Wasiewicz, an elementary school librarian, makes the choosing stage a main focus in her project:

> In the voluntary storytelling club at our school, we spend *at least* the first four months doing nothing but reading—no one makes a choice of a story to learn until after we come back from December vacation. The students do, however, make lists of "possibles" as they read, noting sources (Ah-ha, a bibliography—library reference skills!) so they can relocate the stories later on—(*Wasiewicz*).

Having all students choose a story from their own ethnic heritage is a good idea in theory, but not always a practical one. A number of teachers and librarians have mentioned the difficulties they encountered in carrying out such a project because they were limited to small folklore collections. Even with large collections it is sometimes difficult, or even impossible, to find a story to match the ability level of a younger student. Older students are more likely to be successful with such an assignment, but since even they may encounter difficulty it is better to simply suggest this idea as a possibility.

The more experience you gain with telling stories yourself and with teaching children to tell stories the easier it will be to make judgments about whether a specific student is capable of telling a certain story well. You will encounter both extremes: the student who chooses a story called "The Haunted House" because he likes the title even though he doesn't understand what happens in the story and couldn't begin to tell it; and the student who chooses a story that you suspect will be much too difficult for her, but she surprises you by totally entrancing the class. Those surprises happen because you trusted your students' choices, and they are sometimes worth the mistakes you'll make. Marni Schwartz shared another of her experiences:

> Marla taught me to trust my students' choices of story. She wanted to do *Bambi,* and when we found the original lengthy Bambi text, I doubted she could fashion a telling. She promised me she would do the story justice. What she did, of course, was tell her memory of the Disney movie. But I will never forget the way she created the thicket, the ice-skating scene with Thumper and especially the fire. Marla adapted the telling from her own little girl memories of the movies and every listener in the room relived the journey of Bambi from helpless fawn to forest king—(*Schwartz*).

Each student should tell a different story since the children will be working intensely with the stories, hearing the same story again and again as they listen to their classmates practice. A sign-up sheet will help avoid duplication of stories. Before students choose a story they must consider who their audience will be. If they are eighth graders, for example, they might want to choose a story for primary school children and go to those classrooms; or they might feel more comfortable with a bone-tingling ghost story for sixth, seventh, and eighth graders.

Each student should read at least five stories before choosing one to tell. This process will help them learn to make judgments and comparisons, and also insure that they don't choose the first story they read out of anxiety or eagerness. Before they make a final choice students should *read the story aloud to a partner.* That will help them to see how comfortable they feel with the story, and their partner's reaction may help give them a better idea of whether or not the story is a good one for telling.

If students choose to search for a story which is not in your preselected pool send them to the folk-tale section of the library (Dewey #398.2). Explain that a folk tale would probably be best to choose for telling since these are stories that have been passed by word-of-mouth from one person to another and were only written down relatively recently. They were meant to be told. "Literary stories," or those written by a particular person, were meant to be read. As a result, the language of literary stories often doesn't come across as well when told orally. However, some authors' works are great for telling. The only way to find out is to read the story aloud.

Frequently we work in classrooms in which students are doing a tremendous amount of writing, and teachers wonder if this original material would be appropriate for telling. As we've mentioned, written stories, even by the most experienced of authors, often don't work well when told orally. Since our priority is to have students' first experiences at telling be positive ones, we recommend that they begin by telling a folk tale. Folk tales are meant to be told. They are simple and compelling, and their universal messages make them extremely satisfying for listeners. As students explore folklore in depth they will begin to understand the elements that make a story good for telling. Their subsequent writings are more likely to be suitable for oral presentations.

Be aware that in some picture books part of the story is actually told by the pictures, so unless the teller can add an explanation or change the story easily, it would be best to avoid such a story. (If you have doubts about how the story will come across orally, obviously the best thing to do is to have the student read it aloud to you.)

Consider these points when students bring their stories to you for approval:

1. *Simplicity is essential* if this is to be a rewarding experience for most students. When they bring their stories to you make sure the stories have a simple plot, a minimum of characters, and simple clear language.

2. *The length of the story should be no more than ten minutes.* It is important that stories not be too long so they will be easy to learn, and so that students won't be intimidated about standing in front of a group for a long period of time. If they have success with the first story they learn, they're much more likely to want to learn more in the future. For younger students (second and third graders) and first-time tellers we generally limit the stories to five minutes.

3. *Beware of students choosing stories with dialects.* It takes great skill to do dialects well. Accents can add immensely to the telling of a story, but it is extremely rare for a child to execute them well. In addition, there is the possibility of offending one of the listeners if tellers' accents sound as if they are making fun of a particular ethnic group.

    If tellers choose a story from their own heritage, and feel comfortable using an accent, encourage them to do so. Storytelling provides an opportunity to celebrate the many dialects and idioms that are indigenous to certain areas. The vernacular is often "educated out" of students, but telling a story in their own dialects will allow them to feel proud of their heritage. For example, Appalachian children will enjoy telling "Old Dry Frye" or any of the stories from Richard Chase's *Grand-father Tales*.

Mitch had always wanted to tell the Uncle Remus story, "Brer Rabbit and the Tar Baby," but as a white Northerner he knew he would not feel comfortable using Southern black dialect in the story. After consulting MacDonald's *The Storyteller's Sourcebook* he was able to find a Brazilian version of this story called "Why the Bananas Belong to the Monkeys" which is not written in dialect. He could and did use this version. (Since that time Julius Lester has written two excellent collections of Uncle Remus stories, *The Tales of Uncle Remus* and *More Tales of Uncle Remus: Further Adventures of Brer Rabbit, His Friends, Enemies & Others* which are *not* in dialect.) Again, you will be the best judge of what your students are capable of handling.

When students have chosen their stories, take these next steps:

1. Have them tell you (or write down) the titles of stories they've read and why they've chosen a particular story.

2. For older students you may wish to use the optional "Student Story Sheet" included on the next page.

HANDOUT: STUDENT STORY SHEET (Optional)

Name: _____ Date: _____

The stories I have read are:

_____

_____

_____

_____

_____

The story I have chosen to tell is: _____

I like this story because: _____

_____

_____

The main idea of my story is: _____

_____

_____

List the words or phrases that you don't understand the meaning of, and look up the meanings in the dictionary and list them below:

_____

_____

_____

List the words you do not know how to pronounce:

_____

_____

_____

My story is a: (check one)
☐ fable   ☐ folk tale   ☐ legend   ☐ myth   ☐ fairy tale
☐ tall tale   ☐ literary story (by a specific person)

The country (or culture) my story comes from is _____
(If your story is a literary tale, ignore this question).

Chapter 6

Helping Children Learn Their Stories

CREATING AN AWARENESS OF THE ORAL TRADITION

Before students begin to learn their stories explain what the oral tradition is. In the past stories were always passed on by word-of-mouth and never written down. As the stories were told by different people they changed. You can illustrate the idea that no two people will ever tell a story just the same way by doing this exercise:

EXERCISE: HOW A STORY CHANGES

1. To make your students aware of how one story can be given numerous treatments, tell or read them different versions of the same story. If possible, find audiotapes or videotapes of the same story told by different tellers. A good example would be "Wiley and the Hairy Man," found in these sources:

   Bang, Molly Garrett. *Wiley and the Hairy Man*. N.Y.: Macmillan, 1976.

   Botkin, B.A. *A Treasury of American Folklore*. N.Y.: Crown, 1944 (pp. 682–687).

   Hamilton, Virginia. *The People Could Fly: American Black Folktales*. N.Y.: Knopf, 1985 (pp. 90–103).

   Holt, David. *The Hairy Man and Other Wild Tales* (Cassette tape/Album).*

   Torrence, Jackie. "Wiley and the Hairy Man" is included on *Homespun Tales* (Cassette tape/Album), a collection of stories by various storytellers.*

*See "Storytelling on Video- and Audiocassette" in Appendix A.

2. Tell "The Tailor" by Nancy Schimmel from her excellent book *Just Enough to Make a Story: A Sourcebook for Storytelling.*

THE TAILOR

In a village there once lived a poor tailor. He had made overcoats for many people, but he had never made one for himself, though an overcoat was the one thing he wanted. He never had enough money to buy material and set it aside for himself, without making something to sell. But he saved and saved, bit by bit, and at last he had saved enough.

He bought the cloth and cut it carefully, so as not to waste any. He sewed up the coat, and it fit him perfectly. He was proud of that coat. He wore it even when it was the least bit cold. He wore it until it was all worn out.

At least he thought it was worn out, but then he looked closely, and he could see that there was just enough good material left to make a jacket. So he cut up the coat and made a jacket. It fit just as well as the coat, and he could wear it even more often. He wore it until it was all worn out.

At least it seemed to be all worn out, but he looked again and he could see that there was still enough good material to make a vest. So he cut up the jacket and sewed up a vest. He tried it on, and he looked most distinguished. He wore that vest every single day. He wore it until it was all worn out.

At least he thought it was all worn out, but when he looked it over carefully he saw some places here and there that were not worn. So he cut them out, sewed them together, and made a cap. He tried it on, and it looked just right. He wore it outdoors and in, until it was all worn out.

At least it seemed to be all worn out, but when he looked he could see that there was just enough left to make a button. So he cut up the cap and made a button. It was a good button. He wore it every day, until it was all worn out.

At least he thought it was all worn out, but when he looked closely he could see that there was just enough left of that button to make a story, so he made a story out of it and I just told it to you—(*Schimmel, 1982, p. 1*).

3. After telling this story divide your class into small groups. Have them review the events in the story and then retell it, with each person taking a part. Just continue around the circle until the story is finished. Then have each group retell the story for the class. As they listen to others tell them to observe how each person picks up on certain things and tells the story a little differently.

4. Take this exercise a step further and demonstrate how your class can be just as creative as the tailor by taking the bare bones of the story

and making it into a new one. First, discuss the main ideas in the story:

A. going from big to little,

B. creativity,

C. getting attached to something,

D. being thrifty,

E. object as symbol. The button has become a symbol of the tailor's memories.

> Ask your students if they own an object which has great meaning for them. This could be a wonderful source of stories. Then have them go back to their original groups and make up another story with at least some of the main ideas. (It's helpful, but not essential, to have one parent volunteer for each group to aid students in getting going. If that's not possible, you can wander from one group to the next to help facilitate the process.) If a group seems to be stymied (a rare occurrence; it's more likely that the problem will be deciding on a particular subject because they have *too many* ideas), you may suggest one of these:

> a. A seamstress who sewed curtains (tablecloth, placemats, napkins, etc.).

> b. A person who built a table (bench, chair, stool, cutting board, toothpick).

> c. A person who owned a bus, van, car, motorcycle, bicycle, unicycle.
> (If you just suggest the first object they can probably take it from there.)

5. To further widen students' experience of alternate ways of expressing the story and demonstrating that there is no one right way to tell a story, try these exercises:[9]

A. Tell the story (either the original or the newly improvised one) entirely in mime. This forces students to invent meaningful gestures instead of random handwaving.

B. Tell the story entirely in dialogue. This forces students to put words into the characters' mouths, which livens up a story.

6. A natural extension of this exercise is to have children write their own versions of the stories that they created in number 4 above. Doing the

[9]These exercises were suggested by storyteller Fran Stallings.

oral part of the exercise first allows their ideas to flow quickly and freely. Emphasize that they are not bound by what their group created. If they now choose to create their own unique story they will have had the benefit of hearing numerous other ideas.

These exercises should make your students aware that there are many ways to tell a story, and that each person should find his or her own way. This is especially important to point out to any of your students who choose to tell a story they have heard someone tell either in person or from an audiotape or videotape. They may tend to feel that the way the teller told the story is the "only" way to tell it.

We feel it is wrong to copy word for word, gesture for gesture, nuance for nuance another person's telling of a story. Storytelling is such a personal means of expression that it is the equivalent of stealing another person's creativity to mimic a story exactly. You may think: "But they're just children, and children learn naturally by mimicking." We agree, but feel it's important to encourage children to be creative, and remind them that there is no one "right" way to tell a story. These traditional stories belong to everyone, but each person must put his or her indelible and unique mark on the story. There is an old saying with which Irish tellers often end a tale: "Take this story and may the next one who tells it better it."

GETTING STARTED

Every storyteller has his or her way of learning a story. You will see a number of techniques listed here that we have found to be helpful. Included at the end of this chapter is a sheet of "Suggestions to Help You Learn Your Story." This can be copied and given to students.

THE IMPORTANCE OF PRACTICE

As has been stated earlier, have your students read their stories over and over again. Give them time each day during the project to practice reading the stories. Encourage them to tape the stories if they have a tape recorder at home, and listen to them again and again. The more they practice, the better prepared they will be when they tell their stories in front of an audience. It is best to be very specific and tell them to practice their stories a minimum of three times a day until they feel they know them very well. Then they should continue to go over them at least once a day to keep them fresh in their minds.

Juan works intently on his pictorial outline for "How Coyote Snared the Wind."

METHODS FOR LEARNING

Emphasize that it is not just the choice of words to which they must pay attention. They must become so familiar with the characters and actions in their stories that they feel as if they have actually lived the experiences. It is vital that they are able to "see" their stories as sequences of events. Once they know the sequence they won't fear getting lost as they tell the story. Try these two exercises to get the children immersed in their stories:

*EXERCISE: PICTORIAL OUTLINE

Give this explanation and these suggestions before students begin their outlines:

1. Drawing a pictorial outline will help you "see" your story as a series of pictures. THIS IS NOT AN ART PROJECT! Draw simple/stick figures. Attempting to draw the characters and scenes as you see them in your mind will take too much time. The idea is to do a series of quick, simple drawings that will help you to remember the events in the story in the correct order.

2. Do not draw a series of blank boxes on your paper first. You have no way of knowing how many pictures you will need in order to tell your story. Just think about the first thing that happens in the story, then the next.

3. Again, this is not an art project! Use pencil and don't get too fancy in your drawings. Stick figures are fine. Just like a written outline, this is a rough sketch of your story. Some students get very upset that they cannot draw a particular animal. Most of us can't, and it is not important for this exercise. Tell children to draw the animal as simply as possible and then label it. For example, a wolf might look like this:

4. Sometimes there is important dialogue in your story that you do not want to forget; or perhaps a rhyme that is repeated several times. If you wish to include this in your outline, do it just the way they do it in comic books. Draw a balloon coming out of your character's mouth:

If your character is thinking something important, but not actually saying it out loud, draw three smaller circles coming out of the head, and then draw the balloon:

5. Once you have completed your outline try telling the story just using the pictures. You will find that it will be much easier to tell your story as a series of images rather than as a set of memorized words.

6. When you are finished, go to a designated spot in the classroom. Find a partner who has also finished an outline, and tell your stories to each other, using the pictures you have just drawn.

Here are two examples of pictorial outlines:

SAMPLE PICTORIAL OUTLINE

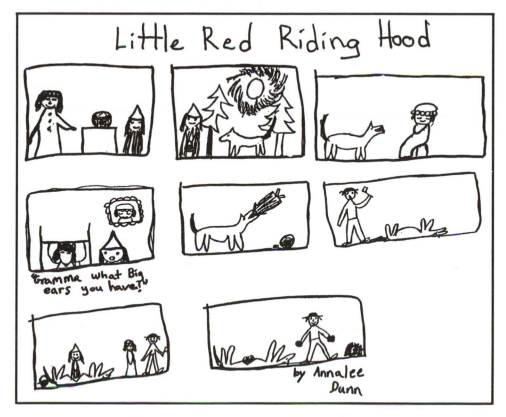

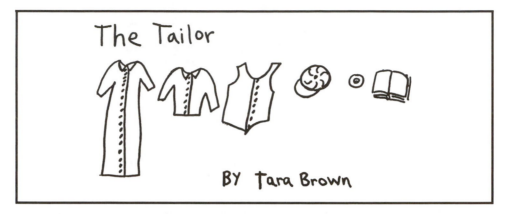

EXERCISE: STORY MAPPING

Another activity that will make students aware of the basic plot line and structure of their stories is "story mapping." They should ask themselves: "What happened first?" And then "What happened after that?" They continue in this way until they've listed all the major events. They should then look for the basic structure (beginning, middle, and end) and any recurring patterns. Their stories may take a linear form or may have a more weblike character. Here's how fourth graders mapped "Little Red Riding Hood" and "The Tailor."

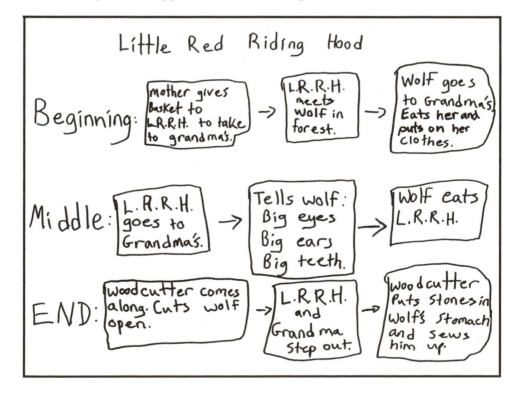

The Tailor

Overcoat → jacket → Vest → Cap → button → Story

BEGINNINGS AND ENDINGS

Stress to your students that the beginnings and endings of stories are especially important:

1. Usually the characters are introduced within the first few paragraphs, the setting of the story is described, and the conflict that is the essence of the story is made clear.

2. The end of a story is essentially like the punchline of a joke. It should be brief, to the point, and final.

3. Although we continually urge children to use their own words in telling stories they may want to consider memorizing the first and last lines of the story. This will allow them to get up in front of the group and begin their stories with confidence. If they have a set ending it will allow them to conclude their stories with self-assurance. Storytellers want their audiences to leave the event with a feeling of satisfaction.

4. One problem that you and your students will encounter is that every story does not have a standard ending, such as "and they lived happily ever after." It is important for tellers to convey to their audiences that the story has ended or they will feel a bit foolish and resort to saying, "The End." This can spoil the effect of the story. Instead, have your students try slowing down and emphasizing the last line of the story. This will let their listeners know that the story is coming to an end. Or when they come to the end of the story they can say, "And that's the story of . . ." We use both of these techniques in our telling and have found them to be quite effective.

LEARNING, NOT MEMORIZING

Emphasize to your students that they are "learning" the story, *not* "memorizing" it. Encourage them to make the story their own; to tell it in their own words. Advise them that they must use simple, powerful language that has the same feeling as the style of the story. Tell them not to use street slang, such as "he goes" instead of "he said" in stories from other places and times, since that will destroy the feeling of "long ago and far away." Words are tools for building a story; they must choose them wisely.

Some students will find it difficult to do anything *but* memorize the story. And you will see that some students who memorize the story will be tense and much more likely to "blank" in the middle of the story when they forget one word. Others who memorize will do a marvelous job and can even sound quite spontaneous. We are not saying that memorizing is wrong; it is a useful exercise in discipline. But we feel children will learn much more if they tell stories in their own words, even if the telling is not as polished as it would have been had it been memorized. As a teacher all you can do is encourage your students every step of the way to make the stories their own, and do the exercises (especially the written and pictorial outlines) that will help them distance themselves from the original text.

EXERCISE: HOW TO IMPROVISE LANGUAGE

All of us are constantly improvising language in our everyday lives. When a friend asks us what we did last night, or when we tell someone a joke we just heard, we use the words we think will be most effective in telling our "story." This is also our task as storytellers. We must use language that will not only describe the events in the story but will also help our listeners to paint pictures in their minds.

When one tells a folk tale one is not tied down by the words on the page. As long as tellers have good mental images of the sequence of events, they will not forget the story. Drawing the pictorial outline should help immensely. It is true that as they tell stories over and over again they may eventually settle into a set way of telling them. As they become more confident they may discover new layers of meaning in the story, and their telling will continue to grow in range. Certainly the more they interact with a live audience, the more spontaneity will creep into the telling.

To give your students a chance to experiment with language, give them a sentence devoid of any description, such as, "The woman lived in the castle." Ask for volunteers to add some adjectives and descriptive phrases that will give different feelings to the sentence, such as: "The *mysterious young* woman lived *all alone* in the *abandoned* castle." Or "The *beautiful* woman lived in *splendor* in the *magnificent* castle." This should be done without too much time for thought. Emphasize that the idea is to improvise, not to come up with a perfect sentence.

IMPROVING ORAL DESCRIPTIVE SKILLS

As our society has become more and more dominated by visual media our oral descriptive skills have become shockingly poor. An ex-policeman recently told us that this is a serious problem in investigative work. Crime victims and witnesses to a crime often have an extremely difficult time in trying to describe the persons they have seen who committed a crime. These exercises will help improve children's oral descriptive skills and make them more comfortable in using language when telling stories.

EXERCISE: DESCRIBING FAMILIAR PEOPLE, PLACES, THINGS

When we ask children to describe a certain character from one of our stories we often get answers like: "She looks just like Madonna." Or "He looked sort of like Freddie Krueger." If we ask them to describe Freddie Krueger their answer is usually, "*You know,* like Freddie Krueger!"

Have your students take a familiar image and pretend to describe it to someone from another planet, or a hermit, or anyone who would have no idea what this person or thing looked like. You can do this all together as a class, or first in small groups and then as a whole.

EXERCISE: SIMILES

To get students thinking more creatively have them complete some similes, such as: "It was so dark on Halloween night that . . . [I couldn't see an inch in front of my face]." Or "He was so tall that . . . [his face was sometimes covered by clouds]." It will not be long before students will supply the entire simile, and perhaps even experiment with them in their stories.

EXERCISE: THE FIVE SENSES

Children are very involved with the five senses. It is through these senses that they learn about the world around them. Stories are filled with sights, sounds, and images that must be conveyed to listeners. The more tellers can immerse themselves in the world of the story, the more believable their telling will become. Storyteller Nancy Schimmel observes:

I use hearing and kinesthetic sense as much as sight in "visualizing" a story. For example, when I tell "The Woodcutter Story," I don't know what color eyes or hair the woodcutter has, and I have only the vaguest idea what he is wearing, but I do know how his body feels to him when I say "At first he walks slowly, scuffing at leaves, but soon he is whistling . . ."; and I know what tune he is whistling—the tenor solo from the choral movement of Beethoven's Ninth Symphony—(*Schimmel*).

To give students a chance to use their senses and then translate them into oral descriptive skills bring in several bags of various spices and herbs. Let the children smell, touch, taste, and look at the spices. Then, instead of having them guess what the spices are, have the children describe them. Some spices that will work well are cinnamon (ground or stick), nutmeg (ground or whole), black pepper (ground or whole), cayenne pepper, turmeric, mustard seeds, or dill weed.

Since you have used only four of the senses (sight, touch, taste, and smell) add an exercise where the children can describe sound. Play several different pieces of instrumental music (jazz, classical, folk, etc.) for your class. You can also look in the library for unusual recordings, such as bird calls, whale sounds, and so on. Then have your students describe what they heard.

WAYS OF PRACTICING

We think the idea of an expanding audience is least threatening to beginning tellers. They start by practicing in front of a mirror or before an imaginary audience, then with a friend or family member, then with a small group of classmates, then to half the class, then the whole class, and so on if they desire (*see* "On the Road to Other Classrooms" in Chapter 8). Here are some specific suggestions:

1. Have your students try telling with an imaginary audience (they can do this in their bedrooms or anytime they are alone). They should look all around the room and not stop while they tell their stories.

2. They might find that telling their stories to a mirror is helpful. This lets them see themselves as their audiences will see them. It also gives them a distraction; they are looking at something as they tell their stories.

3. They should tell their stories whenever they have a chance and to anyone or anything (toys, stuffed animals, pets, plants, etc.) who will listen. In fact, singer/songwriter Holly Near says she began by singing to cows for lack of a better audience. Once students feel they

Lila practices "The Stag and His Reflection" in her mirror.

know the stories they can ask a family member or friend to listen. The listener can use children's written outlines or texts to prompt them with any trouble spots. The more children tell, the more their stories will become a part of them. Telling is the only way to discover the places in the story where their memories fail them. Suggest that students ask practice audiences to point out nervous habits or any other movements that distract listeners from the stories.

4. In your classroom have students first pair off and tell their stories to a partner, then in a group of four, then eight, and so on. Unless your class has already had experience in giving constructive criticism, the listener's role at this point should be just to be a good audience. If you are lucky enough to have adult volunteers or other staff support (one adult for every six to eight kids), you can introduce critiquing at this phase in the project. Our discussion of critiquing is in Chapter 7, "Some Suggestions on Critiquing Student Storytellers." Adults can model what it means to give positive feedback and constructive criticism, and can also step in if children are impolite or negative by interjecting, "That's not an appropriate thing to say."

5. Every storyteller has advice to give about how to learn a story. Here is some from a third grader:

Practice in front of your stuft animals. Then tell it to someone you know like your relitives because you feel more comftible with them and then that will get you going. Also practice in the meror until you know it by hart. You don't have to use the egsact words from the book. You can use your own words.

HANDOUT: SUGGESTIONS TO HELP YOU LEARN YOUR STORY*

1. Read your story out loud over and over again.

2. Make a pictorial outline or story map of the story to help you visualize the sequence of images and events. Then practice telling the story with your pictorial outline/story map.

3. If you have a tape recorder read your story into it and then listen to it over and over again. Listen to your voice for expression, pacing, pauses, and so on.

4. You must learn the plot of your story so that you feel very comfortable telling it. We encourage you to tell the story in your own words. Just be sure to choose simple, powerful language that has the same feeling as the style of the story. For example, don't use street slang (such as "he goes" instead of "he said") in stories from other places and times, or you will destroy the feeling of "long ago and far away." You may want to memorize the first and last lines of your story so that you can begin and end the story with confidence.

5. Character study:

   A. What images take shape in your mind when you try to imagine what the characters in your story are like?

      a. How do they look?

      b. How do they speak?

      c. How do different characters contrast with one another?

   B. Studying characters *does not* mean you will talk more about them or give more description than is included in your story. But it will give you a better understanding of the characters, so that what you *do say* and *movements you make* will be more revealing.

6. Some stories may have a part where the audience can join in. For example, there may be a song or verse which is repeated several times, such as, "I'll huff and I'll puff and I'll blow your house down" from "The Three Little Pigs." Younger children especially love to participate in a story. If you want the audience to help

---

*This handout was designed with students grades five and up in mind. For younger children you may choose to copy it and send it home with the letter to parents so they will have a better idea of how to help their children practice their stories.

you, encourage them by saying, for example, "Please join in on this part." Or "Let's try that together."

7. Summary of ways of practicing:

   A. Try telling with an imaginary audience—look all around the room, and don't stop during the telling.

   B. You might find telling your story into a mirror is helpful. This lets you see yourself as others see you. It also gives you a distraction; you are looking at someone as you tell the story.

   C. Tell your story whenever you get a chance and to anyone who will listen. The more you tell it, the more it will become a part of you. Telling is the only way to discover the places in your story where your memory fails you. Telling your story to listeners will show you other places where you'll want to work to improve your telling. Ask listeners to point out nervous habits or any other movements that distract them from the story.

8. Overlearn your story! Think it through anytime you have a spare minute—while riding the bus, or walking to school, or taking out the garbage. The story will become a part of you and you will feel confident when you get up in front of the group to tell it. Practice your story at least three times a day until you know it, and then once a day to keep it fresh in your mind.

Chapter 7

Helping Children Tell Their Stories

Although there is no one "right" way to tell a story you can give your students guidelines and help them to avoid certain pitfalls. Listed in this chapter are the basic storytelling techniques, and exercises to help illustrate these techniques. At the end of the chapter is a handout on "Techniques to Keep in Mind as You Tell Your Story," which can be copied and given to students.

VOICE

The storyteller's voice is his or her most important tool. It must be filled with expression, always with an awareness of the tone or mood being conveyed to the audience.

EXPRESSION:

Nothing will bore an audience faster than storytellers who do not use a lot of expression in their voices. Ask your students to recall from the stories they've heard recently in class any particular parts where storytellers were especially expressive. Did they sound angry, happy, sad, frustrated, evil, scared, and so on?

EXERCISE: WHAT IS A MONOTONE?

Ask your students if anyone knows what it means to speak in a monotone. Give them an example by telling them a paragraph from a story with no expression or voice variation, and then repeat it using good expression. Discuss their reactions to the two tellings.

*EXERCISE: PUTTING EXPRESSION INTO YOUR VOICE

You can say exactly the same words and, depending on how you say them, give them a completely different meaning. Have students practice saying the following sentences in different ways:

1. "I lost my homework." (sad, happy, frustrated, angry, boasting, nervous, sleepy, rude, apologetic, furious, lazy)

    One variant of this exercise is to hand out cards each of which has a different emotion written on it and have students say the sentence using the assigned emotion. Then have other students try to guess what the emotion is.

2. "What are you doing?"

    a. As if you were furious because you walked into your bedroom and found your brother or sister going through your dresser drawers.

    b. As if you walked into your classroom and found your teacher standing on his or her head.

    c. As if you really weren't interested, but felt you had to ask anyway.

    d. As if you were very suspicious.

    e. As if you were a big mean bully picking on a smaller person.

    f. As if you were a frightened small person who encountered a big bully doing something wrong (even though he or she probably wouldn't ask).

3. Counting from one to ten:

    a. As if you were an angry parent who said, "I'm going to count to ten and if you're not in your bedroom by the time I get to ten you're in big trouble."

    b. As a toddler just learning to count.

    c. As if you were very sad because you thought everyone had forgotten your birthday, but then you walked into your living room and saw ten birthday presents sitting on the floor. How would you count them?

    d. As if you were a referee for a boxing match and you were counting someone out.

    e. As if you were telling someone a telephone number over a bad connection.

    f. As if you were counting pennies as you dropped them into a piggy bank.

    g. As if you were counting the people in a crowded room.

We have invariably found that students cannot get enough of this exercise. They love putting expression into their voices, especially when they get a little "rise" out of their classmates. It is excellent practice for using expression in their own stories. Many students tell us that they fear classmates will laugh at them if they use expression or different voices for their characters. We explain that while it is true some people may laugh during the telling it is only because the teller's enjoyment of the story has been transferred to the audience. If you find that your class responds well to the expression exercise, have them do the next exercise also.

EXERCISE: FEELING AND MOOD

Have your students say any of the following words using the feeling or mood of the word when they say it:

Buzz, clap, grunt, bubble, sniffle, sneeze, blast-off, sleep, splash, gurgle, roar, swish, bang, crackle, wheeze, coo, clang.

EXERCISE: WORD EMPHASIS

By emphasizing certain words, you can completely change the meaning of a sentence. Show the following example to your students, emphasizing the italicized words to convey various meanings:

Did Susan give Dan a red book? (You said so, but did she really?)

Did *Susan* give Dan a red book? (Or was it Jane?)

Did Susan *give* Dan a red book? (I thought it was just a loan.)

Did Susan give *Dan* a red book? (Or did she give it to Joe?)

Did Susan give Dan *a* red book? (I thought she gave him at least two or three.)

Did Susan give Dan a *red* book? (Wasn't it the yellow one?)

Did Susan give Dan a red *book*? (I thought it was a magazine.)

Then ask students to say this sentence, emphasizing different words in it to see how many meanings they can get:

Is Jonathan flying to France this winter?

For older students try this sentence:

I didn't know she went out with him.

VOLUME

Obviously it is very important for listeners to be able to hear a teller clearly at all times. This is often a problem for student tellers. Tell them to focus now and then on the very back row of listeners, and be sure the listeners look as if they can hear well. Robert Rubinstein, a storyteller from Oregon who founded the Roosevelt Troupe of Tellers (a group of middle school students who travel from school to school), has his students tell their stories from inside the classroom closet. They must project loudly enough for everyone in a class to hear (*Rubinstein, 1973, pp. 35–36*).

You must keep in mind the capabilities of each of your students. We worked with a third grader one year who told her story in an almost inaudible voice. We tried a variety of strategies with Julie, including telling her to practice her story as loudly as she could when she was alone in her bedroom. On the day she shared her story before the whole class we huddled around her so that we could hear. But Julie's teacher was extremely pleased with her telling. She informed us that Julie had essentially been nonverbal when she started school. She thought it was an incredible step that Julie had *told her story*. Julie had clearly worked hard and seemed pleased with herself.

Discuss with older students how *breathing from the diaphragm* (the part of the body between the chest and the abdomen) is crucial if they are to be easily heard. Your voice must come from deep in your diaphragm, not from your throat. Have students check for diaphragmatic breathing by using this exercise:

EXERCISE: DIAPHRAGMATIC BREATHING

Lie on the floor on your back and place a book on your diaphragm just above your waistline. The book should rise and fall slowly as you breathe. Now stand up and work for the same movement. Put your hand over your waist and breathe in and out very quickly. Your hand should move out as you inhale and in as you exhale.

Ned tries out his version of "The Lucky Man" on two of his classmates.

TEMPO/RATE

The speed at which you speak should vary throughout a particular story. Speaking more slowly may suggest sadness, suspense, or doubt. Speaking quickly may connote excitement, nervousness, or joy. We usually give the following example from one of our stories: "The Man Who Wasn't Afraid of Anything" is about a braggart who takes a dare to sleep in a haunted house. Where the suspense starts to build the story continues in this way:

> He walked up the creaky stairs and then looked all around the upstairs hallway, and then he opened the bedroom door—CREAK! (*creaky door noise*)

This is said very slowly and deliberately, to convey suspense and make the audience wonder: "What's waiting at the top of the stairs? What's going to be behind the bedroom door?" As the story continues, the braggart grows more concerned about how dark and spooky it is in the house, but he finally relaxes and falls asleep. Then we go on:

(Slowly)	He slept for a while,
(Quickly with fear in our voices)	but then something woke him up. It sounded like something running across the floor. At first his heart started pounding and he got real scared,
PAUSE	
(Gradually get slower and quieter)	but then he realized it was probably just a mouse.
(Very loud, so as to startle the audience)	"A MOUSE!! Of course, that's what it is!" he thought to himself.

Give the brief synopsis and read the excerpts of the story to your students. It is a good illustration of varying tempo as well as volume. You can also show them a storytelling video and have them watch carefully for a very slow or very fast tempo. Afterward have them do these exercises:

EXERCISE: VOICE TEMPO

Repeat the sentence: "The snow is still falling and school has been called off today."

1. Very quickly to convey excitement.

2. Very slowly to show disappointment.

3. At a moderate rate to simply state a fact.

*EXERCISE: THE IMPORTANCE OF SILENCES

Having the courage to pause, simply to be silent for a moment, can be a very effective element in storytelling. Demonstrate this to your students by saying the following sentence:

There was a loud knock at the door, and when she opened it, there stood

(pause)

a strange old man with a long gray beard.

Say the sentence first with the pause, and then try to repeat it exactly the same way except *without* the pause. Then discuss with students what the effect of the pause was. What were they thinking during that instant?

These "pregnant pauses" are very difficult for beginning storytellers. It is not until they have recognized the power that language and corresponding silences can have that they will feel comfortable using them. One technique for overcoming this discomfort is to have storytellers count to three (or whatever) in their heads before opening their mouths to speak. Have them practice incorporating silences into their telling by repeating the sentence you just used in your example. There are numerous spots in any story that you can use for practice; for example, in the story "The Tailor" you can say: "He wore it until it was all worn out . . . (1–2–3). . . . At least he thought it was worn out. . . ." Or in Hans Christian Andersen's story, "The Princess and the Pea," when the princess first arrives at the palace: "The prince opened the palace gates and there stood . . . (1–2–3) . . . a real princess!" After a while children seem to get the timing themselves and drop the internal countdown.

PITCH

The pitch of the teller's voice (highness and lowness) is an excellent tool not only for indicating different emotions (high pitch can connote excitement, being scared, being small; while low pitch can convey strength, self-confidence, disgust, or unhappiness) but also for portraying different characters in a story. Emphasize that it is not necessary for your students to change their voices for each character. There are times, however, when it will feel almost unnatural not to use different voices; for example, a deep gruff voice for the troll in "The Three Billy Goats Gruff." Emphasize that if they do use a specific voice for a character it is essential that they keep the voice consistent throughout their telling of the story.

*EXERCISE: PITCH

The classic example of the use of pitch is "Goldilocks and the Three Bears." Have students in your classroom say: "Someone's been eating my porridge," the way they think Mama and Papa Bear would say it. Then have them say: "Someone's been eating my porridge and they ate it all up!" in Baby Bear's voice. Now have them think about the characters in their own stories. Is it appropriate to change the pitch of their voices for any of them?

EXERCISE: RESPONDING TO AUDIENCE REACTIONS

It is important for students to understand that no two audiences will ever react in the same way. The only way students will really understand this is by telling their stories again and again to different groups. When students first begin to tell stories they often totally ignore the audience. If their listeners laugh they go right on without pausing. To make students aware of the importance of recognizing audience response show them a brief excerpt from a videotape of a live performance by a storyteller or comedian. Be sure to have them pay close attention to audience reaction if you have guest tellers at your school. Tell them to observe how the performer responds to the audience. What would it have been like if the performer had gone right on without waiting until the laughs of listeners had died down?

FACIAL EXPRESSION

Facial expressions tend to come naturally as a storyteller tells a story. If tellers concentrate on putting expression into their voices, corresponding facial expressions will usually follow. This is not to say that storytellers do not have to be aware of their facial expressions. As a teacher you will notice that some tellers are naturally very expressive, while others will have to work hard to show a similar level of vocal and facial expression.

These exercises will help students become aware of the many diversified moods that can be created simply by the expressions on their faces.

EXERCISE: DISPARATE FACIAL AND VOICE EXPRESSIONS

Have members of your class say: "It's nice to see you" in a pleasant voice while trying to maintain an angry expression on their faces. Then have them reverse their facial expressions (pleasant this time) and the mood in their voices (angry). It is extremely difficult to separate one from the other.

Take this exercise a step further by having students try to walk across the room with a happy look on their faces while trying to maintain an angry posture in the rest of their bodies. Then reverse the two moods.

*EXERCISE: PASS THE FACE

Everyone tends to have his or her set patterns of facial expression. In order to help students loosen up and try some different expressions, use this exercise:

> Everyone sits in a circle. You begin by making a face and showing everyone in the circle. Then turn to the person next to you. That person then copies your face and shows it to everyone; then changes to a different facial expression and passes it to the next person, and so on.

Martha and some third graders pretend to walk through a smelly, squishy swamp with tangled vines.

GESTURES AND MOVEMENTS

Whether or not to use gestures can be a very tricky topic with beginning tellers. Some people feel it is best to rely solely on voice and facial expressions when telling a story. In fact, in some storytelling contests students are not allowed to use gestures at all. Although we do feel that voice and facial expressions are of primary importance, gestures can be used to greatly enhance a telling. The secret is that they must come naturally from the teller's enthusiasm about the story, just as they do in everyday speech.

Discuss with your students the fact that they are not in a play and should not act out everything. Although storytelling and theater are related, there are several major differences. In a play all of the images are there before you, whereas with storytelling much is left to the listeners' imaginations. Although actors will tell you that they are very aware of the audience and play to them, there is, nevertheless, the concept of "the fourth wall," which refers to the imaginary wall between actor and audience. Audience members are privy to a scene that is taking place on stage: it is almost as if they are overhearing what is going on.

But with storytelling this barrier is broken down. Storytellers look right into the eyes of the audience, and as they listen, the storytellers disappear as they create images in the audiences' minds.

Another difference between storytelling and theater is that most actors have a single role to play throughout the performance and must remain in character the whole time. Storytellers serve as narrators and all the characters in a story.

The best advice you can give students is to keep their telling simple and do what comes naturally. They shouldn't begin by trying to think up theatrical movements that they can add to their stories. The gestures they do use must help listeners "see" the story better, and not draw attention to the teller. For example, we once had a third grader who fell to the floor as he was telling one of "Aesop's Fables" where a fox trips and falls into a ditch. We explained how his overdramatization caused us to focus on him falling rather than on seeing the fox. It would have been more effective if he had used a simple motion or "jerk" of his upper body (as well as appropriate facial expression) to merely *suggest* that the fox had tripped, thereby allowing his listeners to "see" the image of the fox in their minds.

The problem with student tellers is not usually overdramatization but rather a stiffness in their tellings. Their gestures are frequently confined to unconscious ones that distract and should be avoided, such as playing with their clothes or hair, shuffling their feet, or twisting a ring on their fingers. They must learn to curb these nervous habits so that the movements they do make will be noticed.

Have your students think about what gestures might improve their telling. When they rehearse their stories they should be able to justify and explain any gesture they are using. If they cannot explain it, it should be eliminated. Remember to stress that some stories call for a lot of movement, while others may be better told standing almost perfectly still. They should use gestures only when they feel these will add to their telling.

It is essential to remember that your students are beginning storytellers. It is not until they are comfortable with their voices and facial expressions that they should attempt to bring gestures into their storytelling.

EXERCISE: OBSERVING GESTURES

Ask students to recall from the stories they recently heard in class any particular parts where the storyteller used gestures. Discuss what they liked and didn't like about these movements. In addition, you can play a video of a storyteller and have the students watch carefully for gestures which they feel are either very effective or distracting. The advantage of video is that you can go back and look at it again.

*EXERCISE: PANTOMIME

These exercises are designed to loosen students up and develop their imaginations. They are not meant to encourage overdramatization, but rather to have students see that one uses one's entire body to communicate feelings. There are two basic rules they must follow while doing pantomime:

1. They must know exactly what they're pretending to do.

2. They must not talk unless the exercise calls for speaking.

   A. Everyone stands in a circle. The leader begins by calling someone's name and then an object such as a:

      spider;

      cold, wet, slimy fish;

      china teapot;

      feather;

      dinosaur;

      balloon.

      As the leader calls the name of the object, that object is thrown into the circle using appropriate body movements and facial expressions. The person whose name was called then catches the object, also using appropriate body movements and facial expressions. Then that person changes the object to anything different, calls out someone else's name in the circle, and throws it to that person.

Note: Tell students not to think about this too much; just say the first thing that comes to mind.

   B. We speak with our bodies and faces, as well as our voices. Try saying these sentences without speaking:

      Watch out!

      I'm so cold.

      Come on in!

      I'm not sure of the answer to that question.

      I AM SO MAD!

This is so boring.

That scared me!

Do you really expect me to believe that?

I'm so sorry.

It's really hot in here.

C. Have your class stand in a circle all facing one way. As they begin to walk around the circle call out different situations that will change their walking pattern. The situations are infinite, but here are a few suggestions. Pretend you are walking:

1. home from school knowing that when you get there you will have to do all your chores.

2. across the schoolyard after a foot of snow has fallen.

3. barefoot through a very sticky and squishy swamp.

4. through a blistering hot desert.

5. with your right foot in a cast.

6. through honey.

D. Make a set of cards with one of the following situations written on each. Pass the cards to students who will act them out while their classmates try to guess what it is that they are doing:

1. Sewing.

2. Pretending you're sleepy, but trying to stay awake.

3. Pretending a bee is hovering around you and that you're afraid of it.

4. Opening a jar of pickles with the cover stuck.

5. Washing a window.

6. Brushing your teeth.

7. Drinking a cold refreshing drink on a hot day.

8. Saying "good-bye."

9. Eating a lollipop.

10. Picking apples from a tree.

11. Shivering on a cold morning.

12. Pouring tea and drinking it.

13. Opening a door.

The point of all these exercises is that students should perform these tasks in a believable way. Even if they are using or seeing imaginary things they must believe in them. These exercises are *not* designed to teach children that they should be moving throughout the story but rather to give more power to the movements they decide to use.

EXERCISE: PUTTING IT ALL TOGETHER

This is an exercise that allows your students to incorporate elements of voice, facial expressions, gestures, and movements. Brainstorm—or if you have already discussed the use of voice with your class—review all the different ways you can change your voice:

1. Putting expression into your voice (sad, happy, frustrated, angry, boasting, nervous, sleepy, rude, apologetic, furious, lazy).

2. Emphasizing different words.

3. Changing the volume.

4. Varying the tempo.

5. Using a different pitch.

Now have your class stand in a circle big enough so that they can all see each other clearly. Then have the first student introduce himself by saying, "Hi, my name is . . ." or whatever he wishes. He must use his voice as creatively as he can and make up a movement to go along with his introduction. Everyone in the circle then tries to mimic the voice and gestures of the student. Move around the circle until all the students have had a chance to introduce themselves.

DEVELOPING CHARACTERS

One of the delights of telling stories is that we get to portray all sorts of different characters. In one story a teller may be an evil magician, a ferocious monster, and a brave girl. The storyteller also has to be the narrator. Although it is not necessary for storytellers to make a major transformation for each character in their stories, their tellings will be improved by studying the characters. This *does not* mean they will talk more about their characters or give more description than is included in the stories. But it will give them a better understanding of their characters and make what they do say and movements they do make more meaningful.

These exercises will help give students the insight to add more expression when talking about or portraying their characters.

EXERCISE: CHARACTER STUDY

Have your students pick out the main characters in their stories. They may have several choices, but for this exercise have them choose just one. Then tell them to imagine what this character looks like. Ask them some general questions that will help trigger their imaginations. Tell them that you'll be using "it" to refer to their character no matter what its gender is. Remind them not to giggle or speak, since any noises will distract others from the images they are making. Then ask:

1. What does it look like?

2. What color is its hair or fur?

3. What is it wearing? (Perhaps the character is an animal—have them think about the animal's fur or hide.)

4. How old is your character?

5. What does your character sound like when it speaks?

6. What does your character look like when it walks or runs?

7. What kind of house does it live in?

8. Is your character angry, sad, silly, scared, a bully, shy, mean, or a combination of these things?

Now go around the classroom and have students describe their main characters. Tell your students to walk around the classroom in character. Have them interact with other students' characters. Tell them to think about how their characters would move and how they would talk to others. If you find that your students enjoy this exercise they can do the same thing for other characters in their stories.

EXERCISE: CHARACTER WEB

To continue your students' investigation of their main character(s) have them do a character web. Choosing a character from any story with which they're familiar let students brainstorm a list of the character's qualities. Create

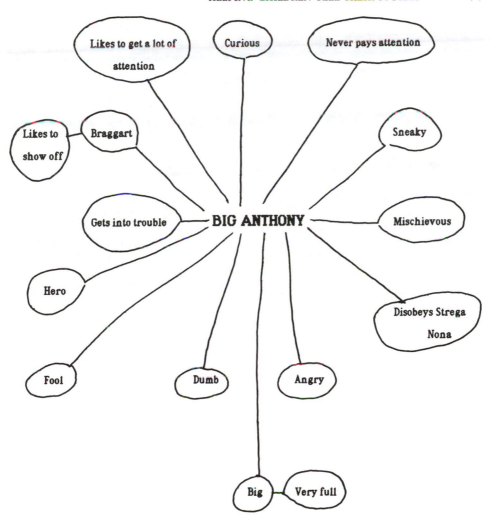

Character web for "Big Anthony" from *Strega Nona*.

a "web" such as we've done for "Big Anthony" from Tomie DePaola's *Strega Nona*. This exercise will also be good for oral descriptive skills, since it will give them a chance to describe their main characters in many ways.

DEVELOPING POISE AND PRESENCE

At the beginning of a play the curtain opens, alerting the audience that something is about to happen. Storytellers must create the same kind of feeling by making eye contact with listeners and pausing a moment to let the audience know they are about to be taken on an adventure to another time and place.

Students enjoy the opportunity to "ham it up" while trying vocal and facial expressions.

Throughout a play actors essentially ignore the audience, but storytelling is a participatory art form. Eye contact with the audience is essential to the close connection made between the teller and the listeners. You will find that you must emphasize this again and again with your students, especially if they have acted in plays where they were told to look just above the heads of the people in the audience. As they watch their classmates tell stories, they themselves will start to notice how different it feels when a storyteller has eye contact and when one doesn't.

You will want your students to begin thinking of how they will go about introducing their stories. Introductions are especially important if students are to sit for several stories in a row. The introduction serves to break the spell of the previous story and allows the audience a chance to tune in to the new teller's voice. The more personal the introduction, the easier it will be for listeners to let go of one tale and move into another.

We always have students practice by introducing themselves (even though everyone in their classroom obviously knows them) because they may eventually be going to other classes where listeners are not familiar with them. Introductions can be as simple as stating the title of the story and/or the country of origin. If it is a literary story, written by a particular author, they must be sure to give the author's name (for example, "The Wishing Well" from *Mouse Tales* by Arnold Lobel). If tellers feel there is more information that would be interesting for their listeners (the collection the story came from or why they chose to tell it, and so on), this can also be included in the introduction. In general, the introduction should not be too long. In fact, some stories are best told with no introduction at all. Tellers certainly don't want to say the name of their stories if it is going to give anything away.

Endings are equally important, and students must be taught how to respond to audience reaction when a story is finished. Instead of rushing to their seats, they must learn how to accept the applause of the audience gracefully.

The exercise below will help students know what to do before they begin their stories and when the stories are over. It is also very helpful for getting them used to the idea of having eye contact with the audience.

*EXERCISE: PRESENCE[10]

Students should walk to the front of the room one at a time and then:

1. Turn to face the audience.

2. Plant their feet solidly on the ground.

3. Scan all the faces in the audience. This should be done with a natural, friendly, and inviting look on the teller's face. To make sure that tellers do not rush this part of the exercise, have them count from one to three in their minds as they look about the classroom. This moment of silence before a story serves several functions and will be particularly important when students actually tell their stories. As tellers make eye contact with their audiences, it is almost as if they are individually welcoming each listener. It also gives the audience a few seconds to focus on the teller and alert their senses that it is time to begin listening.

4. Then say "My name is _____, and I'm going to tell you the story of _____ (name of the story)." Or "My name is _____, and I'm going to tell you a story that comes from _____ (name of the originating country)." Or whatever *brief* introduction the teller has planned.

5. When tellers finish their introductions the audience should pretend they've just finished the whole story, and clap. Tellers then bow as they look at the audience and thank them; then return to their seats.

[10]This exercise was inspired by a similar one created by storyteller Laura Simms.

This is a difficult exercise for children or adults to do well. It is important that you model this exercise for them so they will clearly understand what to do and feel comfortable doing it.

EXERCISE: SUSTAINING EYE CONTACT

If you have students who continue to look at the floor as they tell their stories try this game.[11] Everyone stands in a circle. Explain that you are "it" and you will choose someone from across the circle to trade places with you without saying anything, just by making eye contact; and that you and the chosen person will maintain eye contact while you trade places. Then that person is "it" and chooses the next person by eye contact, trades places, and so it goes. Once they catch on you can split into two or three groups so it doesn't take forever for everyone to get a turn. Be sure to tell them they must choose someone who has not yet been chosen until everyone has had a turn.

At the end of the exercise point out how much power eye contact had during the game, and remind them that it has a great deal of power in storytelling too.

COPING WITH STAGE FRIGHT

Storytelling will be no different from any other new class activity in that some will take to it naturally and relish the chance to "perform" for their classmates while it will be much more difficult for others. One of the biggest concerns will be stage fright. As one second grader wrote: "At first I was so embarrassed. I thought everybody would laugh and say, 'Boo, that stinks,' but they didn't."

The nervous energy one feels during a performance is perfectly natural; it is the body's attempt to deal with a new and exciting situation. The task of storytellers is to use this extra energy to become more dynamic and infuse life into their stories, to let the energy work for them rather than against them. Storyteller Heather Forest suggests: "If young tellers are nervous, I reassure them that although the audience may be looking at them, almost mesmerized by them, the storyteller disappears as the listeners watch the tale unfold in their own imaginations."

The more you talk about these anxieties in the classroom the greater chance there is that your students will feel more comfortable in telling their stories. Share with them your own experiences of feeling nervous—perhaps your first day of teaching school or something from your own school days. This is another discussion that may elicit many stories from your class. They

---

[11] Suggested by storyteller Nancy Schimmel.

will soon be telling about when they've been nervous in different situations.

Remind them that everyone has been given the same assignment. When someone gets up to tell a story, that person is facing a roomful of sympathetic listeners. They know how hard the student has worked on the story and will give the teller their best attention. This supportive atmosphere will go a long way in helping to dissipate stage fright.

In the beginning stages of the project you may worry that some of your students will never be able to tell in front of an audience. We feel that you will be surprised, however, for again and again teachers have remarked to us how astonished they were to see students work through their nervousness. As one fourth grader commented: "When I got up to tell my story, I was nervous like crazy. My knees felt like falling off, but I liked it. I learned not to be afraid on the stage when telling my story. Now I want to tell stories to the younger kids and maybe even the older ones too."

HOW TO DEAL WITH BLUNDERS

Even seasoned professional tellers make mistakes now and then during the course of a story. Let your students know that it is only natural to stumble over a word here and there, especially when they're just beginning and are not yet very familiar with the story. Frequently, listeners are so involved in a telling that they don't even notice a little mistake like saying "him" instead of "her," and so on. Tellers should correct the mistake if they think it's necessary and then go on. *Never apologize to the audience!* This only calls attention to the mistake and makes the audience uncomfortable. If tellers laugh at themselves and take everything in stride the audience will remain relaxed and continue to enjoy the story.

We have actually seen stories which were *improved* by a mistake because tellers laughed at their blunders and then made a comment that somehow put the audience at ease. One fifth grader was telling "The Lucky Man" from Maria Leach's *The Thing at the Foot of the Bed* in which a man shoots his night shirt that is hanging on the clothesline in his back yard, all the time thinking that it is a ghost. The boy telling it said: "He shot it five times; no, it was ten times." Then he laughed and said: "Well, in any case, he shot it a lot of times." His lighthearted handling of this mistake reminded his listeners that we're all human, and strengthened the bond between teller and listeners.

THE USE OF PROPS

We never use props ourselves, not because we feel it's wrong to use them but because they provide images and thus keep listeners from being able to create their own pictures in their minds. Since most of today's kids have few chances to use their imaginations, we feel it's important to provide them with as many opportunities as possible to do so.

Because we don't use props, kids with whom we've worked have never asked if *they* could. If they had, we would probably have been very hesitant to say yes, partly for the above-stated reasons, as well as the fact that props are difficult to use effectively. Unless they are used well they end up distracting from the story rather than adding to it. If your students have seen a teller who uses props well, they will be more likely to want to use props themselves. Because they have had a model they will also be more likely to do a good job. If the issue of props should come up in your classroom you will have to decide what guidelines you wish to set.

SOME SUGGESTIONS ON CRITIQUING STUDENT STORYTELLERS

Teaching someone to tell a story can be tricky because it is an art and therefore a form of personal expression. Nevertheless, by giving students suggestions for specific aspects of technique (for example, eye contact, vocal expression, and so on) you will help improve their telling greatly. Always give positive feedback first, and follow with constructive criticism. Be kind with your criticism and sensitive to the fact that telling a story, especially for the first time, is not easy for most people. Storytelling is also different from a written assignment because it is there for everyone to see. As a result the potential for embarrassment is great. It is vital that your students are constantly being encouraged and that their best efforts, however mediocre, are supported and applauded. Devise a list of things that you can say to even the least successful storyteller, such as:

"That was a good effort!"

"Your voice was loud and clear."

"You knew your story very well. I can see you've practiced."

"You kept your hands (or feet) still as you told the story."

"You did a good job of keeping eye contact with the audience."

Since critiquing can be such a sensitive process it may be best in the beginning, or even throughout the entire project, to do critiques in small groups while the rest of the class is involved in silent work or in other small group activities. A smaller critique session will be a much less threatening environment in which children receive feedback. It will also be easier to retain the interest of listeners in the group if they hear only a few stories at a time.

1. Right from the start you will want to discuss with your class what it means to be a good audience. In the course of a storytelling project each student will be doing a lot of listening, so it is important to lay down the ground rules. Remind them that they will want their class-mates to be quiet and attentive when they tell *their* stories, so they should do the same for others. Because it's hard to listen for long peri-ods break the stories up with a song, stretch, or other participatory ac-tivity. Another way to pause between stories is to take a snapshot of the teller in a favorite pose from the story. Mount these on a bulletin board in the school to let everyone know about your storytelling project.

2. We have already discussed the nervousness that almost everyone in the class is going to experience. Tell your students that sometimes when people are nervous they do things they don't even realize they are doing, such as shuffling their feet, clearing their throats, or playing with their clothes or hair. These nervous habits are distracting when a person is telling a story. Let students know you will point out these habits and help them to avoid them. If children move their hands too much, or play with their clothes, have them put their hands behind their backs. If that fails, have them stand behind a chair with their hands on it.

EXERCISE: RELAXATION

Before each storytelling session you may want to lead the class in a short relaxation exercise. It's quite silly and should put them all at ease. Have everyone take a deep breath and raise their hands over their heads. As they exhale, they should drop their hands and shake their hands and heads with a loud "AHHH!!" as they feel the tension leaving their bodies. You can use this exercise anytime you see that one of your students is telling in a stiff and nervous manner in front of the class. Have the whole class do the exercise together.

3. To keep listeners involved, enlist their aid in critiquing. It provides a good opportunity for children to be generous with one another. But again you must lay down the ground rules right from the start:

   A. It's not okay to laugh at someone's telling unless it's funny.

   B. "Put downs" are not acceptable.

   C. Whatever you say must be positive, and said in a way that will help tellers the next time they tell a story.

If you have never utilized your students as fellow critics you may be in for a pleasant surprise. Teachers have frequently remarked that they were amazed by how kind children were to one another. They saw a spirit of cooperation in the classroom that eventually extended to other projects. Part of this stems from the fact that there is a hierarchy in most classrooms in terms of academic ability. However, it is not necessarily the academically gifted who excel at storytelling. The project will allow students to see their classmates in a different light.

One of our closest friends is a third grade teacher who has become passionate about teaching writing in his classroom. He uses the writing process approach (based on the research of Lucy Calkins, Don Graves, Don Murray, and others) in which there is always a point where the writer receives feedback from fellow writers. To prepare students for this process, he first shows students how to critique. He makes up an absolutely terrible story and reads it to the class. If their feedback runs along the line of "your story was stupid," he gets a hurt look on his face, discusses the consequences of their remarks with them, and asks them how they could have helped him improve his story without hurting his feelings.

You can use this process of modeling to prepare students for their critiquing role. Try telling part of "The Tailor," or the story you are working on, in several different ways, and have students analyze your telling. First tell part of the story with good expression, but don't look at your class. Stop and ask them what they thought of how you told the story, making sure they give positive feedback and then constructive criticism. Tell another part of the story looking at them as you tell it, but talking in a monotone. It won't take them more than a few sentences to pick up on what you need to improve. The more chances you give your students to help one another, the more sensitive and caring they will become.

After a student has shared her story with the class begin by asking: "What's one good thing you noticed Susan did when she told her story?" Eventually you can say: "Now what can Susan do to make her story even better?" It is a good idea to make notes as you go and attach a small sheet of paper to each student's story listing "Things We Liked" and "Things to Work On."

4. You will often need to help children to be more expressive. For example, if a child tells a story with a hungry fox seeing a goose and saying: "That looks like a tasty dinner," in a monotone with little facial expression, you might stop them and ask: "Now how would a hungry fox *really* say that? What sort of expression would he have on his face?" If this doesn't bring results you may want to ask: "What's your favorite food? Why don't you pretend you're starving and that the goose is, for

example, a pizza and say: 'That looks like a tasty dinner!' the way you might in that situation?" If the teller continues with the same unconvincing voice and facial expression, have other students join in. For example, say: "At the count of three, why don't we all say, 'That looks like a tasty dinner!' the way a hungry fox would?" This will help the teller relax and will usually bring about improvement.

5. Children often rush through their stories. If children start off too quickly have them stop, and along with everyone in the class take a couple of deep breaths and start over, *more slowly*. When the audience laughs, you will need to remind tellers to wait before proceeding, or their listeners won't have enough time to enjoy the moment and also won't be able to hear if others are still laughing. There's really no way to learn this except by practice. The more tellers become familiar with the story, the better they'll be at anticipating audience reaction.

6. If students say they just don't know their stories we usually have them come to the front of the room anyway. We then tell them to give us a copy of the story or story map and offer to help if they have trouble. We've found that often children really *do* know their stories, and when they're gently coaxed and actually come up they do a fine job. Have tellers do as much as they can, and if they really don't know the story well enough to tell it, ask them to summarize the rest. Tell such students you expect them to practice and that you'll give them another chance tomorrow.

7. A video camera is a helpful tool to use in conjunction with critiquing, since it allows students to see exactly what they are doing. Explain that everyone, professional storytellers included, is very disconcerted when he or she first sees himself or herself on videotape. After the initial shock, students should be able to pick up many pointers from watching themselves.

8. If you have students who ramble on to the detriment of the story, have them go back to their original outlines and practice telling the story in its most basic form to remind themselves what is really important in the story. Then give them a time limit, and tell them they'll have to figure out how to tell the story within that time frame. This is not a common problem but one we have encountered a few times.

9. It is important to give tellers a chance to work through their mistakes as they tell the story. Don't be too quick to jump in and rescue them if they start to flounder. It can be difficult watching a student struggle through a section of a story, but, as Marni Schwartz found, some gentle guidance may be all that is needed:

Joanna got stuck in the middle of the telling. I watched her let the audience invade her concentration and then she couldn't go on. She looked at me with an expression of panic. The class was very respectful. Some looked at her; some looked toward me to see what I would do. Everyone stayed quiet. I just nodded my head as if to say "You can do it." When that didn't help after a bit, I whispered (from the back of the room), "Go back inside the story. Boots and his brothers were walking through the woods, and . . ." It took her a second but she let go of her panic and did step back inside the story. A few other times during the tale she seemed to start to slip out but my nodding and silent gesturing seemed to reassure her that we were listening and wanted the rest of the tale. All my students learned that day what it means to keep your concentration inside the story, and I think my retelling of what happened to Joanna has helped my students in years since—(*Schwartz*).

JOURNALS

Students can be encouraged to keep a journal throughout the project. They can write about the process of choosing a story, their fears, or how their tellings changed. Marni Schwartz shared some of her students' journal entries:

I found myself saying all these new things I had never practiced. It was like I was in the story and seeing the place of it and seeing things I had never seen before.

I know I can tell my story funny or sad. I wonder which way the audience will want me to tell it?

Well, I was still nervous in my final telling. I got really sweaty. But no one laughed at me.

When I watched Brian tell his story it made me want to tell mine with gestures. He really made it funny by all he did, especially when he said little things to the audience as if he weren't on stage for just a minute.

I'm getting to like my story. I'm finding you can make friends with your story and then you want to tell it well to give it dignity.

PHYSICAL SETTING

Interruptions are a fact of life in the school day, making it difficult to absorb your class in a project. It will be especially disruptive to the teller, as well as to listeners, if people are entering and leaving your classroom or if the loudspeaker comes on. Try to make the actual telling of stories a special time. Perhaps there's an area in your room that you use for reading that can double as the storytelling area. You could begin each session with a little ritual to let everyone know that the magic is about to begin. The New York City Public Library has a tradition of lighting a candle to signify the beginning of the story hour. Perhaps your class can come up with its own tradition.

To avoid interruptions you may want to put a STORYTELLING IN PROGRESS sign on the door. Do not underestimate how much a quiet setting can influence the activity. Of the many storytelling performances that we have given, the ones that were least successful almost always had to do with a problem in the setting. We have encountered gyms with horrendous acoustics, or even a class going on behind the divider; cafeterias with noisy freezers; and auditoriums with stages that separated us from our audiences. Storytelling is an intimate art and deserves the best setting that you can find.

In Chapter 8, "A Celebration of Stories," we suggest an evening performance of volunteer tellers for family and friends. Again it is important you consider the setting. If there is a room in your school that has a nice ambiance—perhaps the library—you may want to have the evening session there. No matter where you have it, be sure the audience is seated with its back to the entrance of the room. That way they will not be distracted by people coming and going, which frequently happens at performances where there are lots of little children in the audience. Try to be sure that the background behind the teller is not too distracting. For example, erase what's on a chalkboard directly behind a teller. Try to place yourself in the shoes of the tellers and see if there is anything else you can do to make the tellers as comfortable as possible.

HANDOUT: TECHNIQUES TO KEEP IN MIND AS YOU TELL YOUR STORY*

1. *Your Voice Is Your Most Important Tool.*

    A. *Put expression into your voice.* Make your voice sound angry, or frightened, or sad, or frustrated, and so on. Nothing will make listeners lose interest more quickly than someone speaking in a monotone.

    B. Although you should always *speak loudly enough,* so that all your listeners can hear you, you must be sure to vary the volume of your voice. Sometimes you may speak louder for effect; at other times softer.

    C. *Vary your rhythm or tempo.*

        a. Try not to rush *or* go too slowly when telling the story.

        b. When there's a lot of exciting action you'll want to speak more quickly. When events are urgent speak of them with urgency. But there are times when you will want to speak slowly to create a feeling of suspense and anticipation.

        c. *Be brave enough to use silence* when it's called for. This can be the most effective moment in a story. It creates intensity and allows the listener a chance to breathe.

2. *Eye-to-Eye Contact.*

    It is very important that you look at your listeners as you tell the story. This makes them feel involved in the story and you will be able to see enjoyment of the story in their eyes.

3. *Gestures May Be Used to Enhance Your Story.*

    Keep gestures simple. Remember, you are *not* acting in a play where you act out everything that happens. In storytelling you only try to suggest what's happening in the story with simple gestures that come naturally to you, such as:

    > She pointed to the moon in the sky. (Point over the heads of the audience and pretend to actually see the moon.)

---

*This handout was designed with students grades five and up in mind. For younger children you may choose to copy it and send it home with the letter to parents so they will have a better idea of how to help their children practice their stories.

Some stories will call for gestures more than others. Remember that any gestures you use should help listeners create better pictures in their minds, *not* cause them to focus more on you.

4. *Beginnings.*

Don't just dash to the front of the room and rush into your story. Walk up with confidence and find your place. Feel your feet on the ground. Look around at your audience, and then say: "My name is _____, and I'm going to tell you the story of _____," or any appropriate introduction.

5. *Endings.*

A strong ending will leave your audience feeling that the story had power. Finish the story with assurance. Wait for the audience to acknowledge your performance before returning to your seat. Take a short bow if you'd like, and say, "Thank you." If you feel your story does not have a conclusive ending you may need to pause a second and say something like: "And that's the story of _____."

6. If you forget a part of your story don't panic or apologize. It's better not to say anything, since that won't upset the flow of your story. Just pause, picture where you are in the story, and then go on. You may feel more confident if you give a copy of your story to your teacher before you go up to tell it, so that the teacher can prompt you if you forget.

HANDOUT: STUDENT SELF-EVALUATION (GRADES FIVE AND UP)

Ask yourself these questions after the first few tellings of your story:

1. Did I choose a story which is appropriate for the age level I plan as the audience? Ask for feedback from your teacher and classmates on which grades they think would enjoy your story.

   _____

2. Was my introduction satisfactory? _____

   Do I need to make it shorter or longer? _____

   Did I fail to mention anything which would help listeners understand the story better?

   _____

3. Do I know my story well? Are there any parts I need to review?

   _____

4. Did I begin the story with confidence?

   _____

5. Did I maintain eye contact with my listeners?

   _____

6. Did I speak loudly enough for everyone to hear?

   _____

7. Did I speak clearly enough for everyone to understand?

   _____

8. Did I use good expression? _____

9. Are there any simple gestures which might add to the effectiveness of my telling?

   _____

   If I used gestures, were they simple ones which helped my listeners create pictures in their minds?

   _____

10. Did I appear to be relaxed and calm, or did I use distracting mannerisms such as pulling on my clothes, playing with my hands, or rocking my feet?

_____

11. How was my pacing? _____

Were there times when I should have slowed down or speeded up?

_____

12. Are there any parts of the story where I might want to ask listeners to join in?

_____

What could I say to make it clear that I want them to help?

_____

Should I ask them at the beginning of the story or just before I want them to participate?

_____

13. If I made mistakes, how did I react? _____

_____

Was the audience aware of my mistake? _____

Could I have handled the situation better? _____

If it happens again, what should I do? _____

_____

14. Did I finish the story with a strong ending? _____

Did listeners know the story was over? _____

If not, what can I do next time to make it obvious that I am finished?

_____

_____

Chapter 8

A Celebration of Stories

ON THE ROAD TO OTHER CLASSROOMS

Once children have learned the stories and shared them in your classroom the celebration of what they have learned can begin. Arrange for students to go in small groups and tell stories to the younger children in other classes in your school so that they will have many opportunities to really perfect their telling and grow more comfortable in front of groups. Encourage them to go to upper-grade classrooms as well. The more they tell, the better they'll be and the more confidence they'll gain. As one fourth grade student wrote: "I would even like to learn another story and maybe another one after that so I can tell a lot of stories to people and make them laugh or maybe they'll learn something. I like to make people feel good."

As they go from class to class, they'll find that audience reactions will be somewhat different each time.

> Kristin had told her version of Dr. Seuss's *Yertle the Turtle* many times to her peers. She delivered the story in a very adult way, but when I sent her to a kindergarten class she told me upon her return, "It changed! I found myself moving closer to them, and saying things, like 'And do you know what happened next?' That just came out of my mouth!" She seemed to discover the hunger for story in a group of young language users, and she didn't disappoint them—(*Schwartz*).

Kristin had made an important discovery concerning the art of story-telling: Learning a story is not the end of the process. As audience reactions change so will the telling. Every new audience provides a different set of challenges for the teller. Try to provide your students with fresh listeners so they will continue to grow with their stories.

Jayme shares Joy Cowley's "Cheer Up, Dad" with a group of appreciative senior citizens.

COMMUNITY TELLING

Schools are one of the greatest resources of a community. And yet all too often many community members are unaware of the wide variety of activities that go on in schools. Taking your storytellers out into the community will not only be good for public relations but also be a chance to share the joy of storytelling with a much wider audience. There are a number of organizations that would be delighted to hear your storytelling troupe. Arrange for your students to visit senior citizens' homes and associations, service organizations, other schools, and the public library. If your community has an annual fair or festival try to arrange for your class to take part.

Our hometown has a three-day celebration every June. Now that we are teaching storytelling in the local schools we plan to bring a group of tellers to the festival. One thing that you must be very careful about when you take your show on the road is that the setting be as optimal as possible for storytelling. You must insist on a quiet spot for the benefit of your tellers and their listeners. Fairs and festivals can be difficult, but if a secluded spot a bit removed from all the main action can be found, or if the storytelling will be the only thing happening in that time slot, then by all means arrange for your students to take part.

CONTESTS

Some school districts have sponsored storytelling contests. These serve to arouse a lot of student interest and can help children learn how to deal with disappointment and to accept defeat as well as victory. There are several counties in New York State that have been running successful contests for years. The Board of Cooperative Educational Services (BOCES) in the state organizes the contests. If you do not have the benefit of a similar organization in your home state Barbara Budge Griffin's book, *Student StoryFest—How to Organize a Storytelling Festival*[12] will give you basic details on how to organize a contest.

It is important to consider all the pros and cons before deciding to hold a contest. It is true that a contest will generate a great deal of excitement, and the final evening of telling, where the winners are chosen, makes for a wonderful community event. Yet contests do, by their very nature, arouse a competitive spirit that may foster the idea that winning is all important and that nothing is worth learning or working at unless there is a prize involved. In speaking of his work with children as poets Byron Padgett states: "I discourage the kind of competitiveness that makes most kids feel anxious, unloved, and defeated, or vainly victorious. I do not single out the 'best' works. Creativity should not be turned into a contest"—(*Padgett, 1976, p. 61*).

FESTIVALS

As an alternative to a contest we propose having a storytelling festival in your school. With a storytelling "festival," as opposed to a contest, children learn to tell stories for the sheer enjoyment of sharing with others. Because they are not competing, there is much better development of peer support and camaraderie within the classroom. There are many forms that a festival can take. Perhaps it will be a time that you put aside in your classroom for all the students to tell their stories. Or if several classrooms in your school are involved in the project you can all join together for a morning or afternoon of storytelling.

For the past three years we have worked with three third grade teachers in Norwich, New York. Each year, on our last day at the school, we had an all-day

---

[12] To order a copy write Barbara Budge Griffin, 10 South Keeneway Drive, Medford, OR 97504, (503)773-3306.

storytelling festival. All three classrooms gathered for three one-hour sessions of telling. The tellers were strictly volunteer, and by the end of the day even students who did not originally volunteer had their hands up asking to be the next teller.

Teachers can get together and decide on a method for selecting tellers. You can try to include *all* the volunteers, but this may not be possible. With a large group of listeners it is important to choose students who will be able to keep the attention of the group. We feel it's also important to choose students who have worked hard to learn their stories, and especially those who have really overcome hurdles and surprised everyone in the class by their tellings. During the sessions you may want to include a song or a stretch to give listeners a break.

It's a good idea to have students use a microphone when telling before a group larger than classroom size. This will give tellers more confidence and make it easier for listeners to hear those students who do not project well. A lavaliere or clip-on microphone would be best if you have access to one. Once the microphone is clipped on it is as if students are telling without a microphone. They do not have to worry about it. If you use a stand-up or hand-held mike it will be necessary to practice with one beforehand so that your students will be at ease using it. Unfortunately, stand-up or hand-held mikes can be inhibiting for those students who use actions in their storytelling.

We ended each year in Norwich with a party in the cafeteria. In another school, Enfield, where we have worked extensively, teachers gave their students certificates when they told their stories on festival day. This was a school where every child got to tell a story, so there were no children who did not receive a certificate. It was a way of congratulating students for participating in the Enfield School Storytelling Festival and was a tangible reminder of all the hard work they had put in on their stories.

PARENTS' NIGHT

When you feel that your students have acquired sufficient experience in telling their stories a great way to culminate the project is to have an evening performance for family and friends. We have always done this on a strictly voluntary basis since it will probably be the students' most difficult audience. They will not find a more supportive or responsive audience, but just telling to adults, especially when the audience includes their families and friends, may unnerve some students. There will be those who will rise to the occasion and tell the story better than ever before and others who will actually regress.

We recommend giving your class a pep talk before the evening performance. A discussion of their anxieties should put them at ease, and if nothing else happens will let them see that many of their classmates are experiencing

Beckie engages the attention of children and parents with her telling of "The Legs."

the same feelings. Explain to them that adult reactions may be quite different from what they're used to. For one thing this will be the first time the adults have heard many of the stories, except for their own child's. They will be hearing the stories with a fresh outlook, unlike the students who have heard the stories over and over again. Also adults may laugh at certain parts that their classmates never have found amusing. Stress to your tellers that the audience is not laughing at them but just showing their enjoyment of the stories and the tellers.

A number of parents have said that the evening of stories has always been overwhelmingly positive. Not only do they have the chance to see their children as the center of attention as they tell their stories but they also get a chance to listen to an evening of stories, an experience most of them probably have not had since *they* were children. Many of them are surprised that they are drawn to these simple stories and are equally surprised by how enjoyable they find the evening. But by far the most common reaction the parents have is their amazement that their children could actually "perform" for the evening gathering. As one parent said: "I can't believe my daughter just got up there all by herself and told her story in front of a whole group of people. She didn't even seem scared. I would have been terrified!"

We suggest giving parents a copy of the handout "Keeping Storytelling Alive at Home" (*see* next page) after parents' night, in the hope that they will begin to build on storytelling traditions which exist in their families, and to forge new ones as well.

It is inspiring to see children confidently telling their stories before an audience. Several teachers who had initially been reticent about telling stories were so impressed by their students that they went on to learn their first stories. Students have also been inspired by other students. One of our most rewarding experiences was working with separate groups of fourth, ninth, and twelfth graders in one school district. We arranged for some of the ninth graders to observe some of the fourth graders, who were so much more expressive and uninhibited, tell their stories at an evening performance. Afterward the ninth grade teacher said that her students were amazed by how good the fourth graders were. One of them said: "Boy, those kids were great! They used gestures; they looked at us; they weren't *afraid* like we are. But I remember when I was their age. I wasn't afraid either." And the ninth grade teacher had replied: "Don't worry. It will pass."

We were pleased to see that the ninth graders had learned more than just how to tell a story. They had also learned that the awkwardness of adolescence is only a phase. Later we noticed that the ninth graders were willing to take more risks when they told their stories.

HANDOUT FOR PARENTS: KEEPING STORYTELLING ALIVE
AT HOME

Stories are an integral part of family life. They have always been used for entertainment, to pass on family history, to teach lessons, to initiate new members into the family, and to put children to sleep at night. Stories are part of the "glue" that binds families together. These suggestions and sources can help you to enrich your family storytelling traditions.

1. Begin simply by reading stories aloud. Stories appeal to the imagination, allowing listeners to create their own images in their minds as opposed to television or other media where all the images are made by others. A very helpful resource is Jim Trelease's *The Read-Aloud Handbook* (N.Y.: Penguin Books, 1985). It includes an annotated list of more than 300 of his favorite books to read aloud.

2. Take it a step further and try putting the book away and telling your children some stories. You will find a whole new intimacy develops, along with the kind of enchantment that occurs around a campfire. Try to remember the stories you heard as a child. You will find a wide selection of stories from around the world in the folk tale section of your public library. A very useful source is Anne Pellowski's *The Family Storytelling Handbook: How to Use Stories, Anecdotes, Rhymes, Handkerchiefs, Paper, and Other Objects to Enrich Your Family Traditions* (N.Y.: Macmillan, 1987). You can also make up your own stories. Once you get a story started, you will find that your child will supply you with ideas whenever you get stumped. Bedtime, long car rides, and holiday celebrations provide excellent opportunities for the sharing of stories.

3. A rich source of stories is your own life and that of your family. Tell the children about events in your childhood, such as your first day of school, scary adventures, practical jokes, vacation escapades, how your ancestors came to this country, or how your family got its name. In this way your children will learn about you, and they will also be discovering their heritage and building links with their pasts. An excellent book on the subject of family stories is *A Celebration of American Family Folklore,* Stephen J. Zeitlin, Amy J. Kotkin, and Holly Cutting Baker, editors (N.Y.:

Pantheon, 1982). It is chock full of stories which will help you trigger memories of your own family stories.

4. Frances Moore Lappé's *What to Do After You Turn Off the TV* (N.Y.: Ballantine, 1985) is full of creative ideas for enjoying family time. The author describes all sorts of activities, from simple games to storytelling to arts and crafts that can become a whole new basis for family interactions. Try turning off the television in your house for a week and see how much fun you can have.

Chapter 9

Helping Children Develop Family and/or Experience Stories for Telling

An effective way of emphasizing that we are all storytellers is through the use of family or experience stories. Mitch has a favorite story which his mother likes to tell and which he often shares when we do adult programs:

> Every Sunday when I was growing up my paternal grandparents used to come for dinner. These family gatherings were welcomed by everyone except my mother, who was stuck making an elaborate meal for her in-laws. This would not have been so bad except that my grandfather was a very difficult man to please. He always had a comment to make about her cooking.
>
> Now one afternoon my mother and grandmother were preparing a tongue for supper. That's right—a nice big, juicy cow's tongue. To cook tongue you simply place it in a pot of boiling water with a few seasonings. As the tongue cooks, every so often a layer of scum comes to the surface. On that Sunday my mother and grandmother carried the pot upstairs to the bathroom to pour out the old water. But while they held the pot over the toilet bowl the entire tongue plopped into the bowl. Since the bowl was clean and they were going to boil it for another forty-five minutes they just rinsed off the tongue, placed it back in the cooking pot, and put in clean water. My mother was worried, however, about my grandfather's keen sense of taste.
>
> Time came for supper. My father sliced up the tongue and placed slices on everyone's plate. My grandfather took one bite of that tongue, and then put his fork down and declared: "This is the most delicious tongue I've ever tasted!" And my grandmother quickly replied: "Don't worry, Morris, I know the recipe!"

We encourage teachers, especially those who are hesitant to learn a folk tale, to tell stories about themselves to their classes. Students have a difficult time imagining their teachers were ever as young as they are, and are shocked to find the teachers have lives outside of school. One school librarian told us that she opened her door on Halloween night to find one of her students at the door. The child, who looked very surprised, asked: "What are *you* doing here?"

Third graders share their stories with partners.

At another school a teacher said the school secretary opened her door to a group of trick-or-treaters, all of whom attended her school. They instantly grew silent as children often do when they see an adult who has escaped from the school. They seemed to be trying to peer behind the secretary, as if they were looking for someone or something. She asked: "What are you looking for?" One of the students replied: "Where's Mr. Manley?" He was the principal of the school, and the student had assumed that since he and the secretary were always together in the office they must live together at home as well. Our point is that your students will be delighted to hear stories from your past, a past they cannot fathom.

Students are also especially interested in telling their own experience stories, or collecting stories from family members and friends. By doing this they establish a link with their pasts, and also gain a sense that the knowledge brought to school is as valuable as that which they take from it.

Storyteller Mary-Eileen McClear has noted:

> What better way to foster self-esteem than by encouraging students to tell stories of their own lives and of their families. I have heard stories that

range from refugee immigration to a darkly humorous account of a near drowning to real life ghostly encounters and even to being stuck in a laundry chute! The structuring of anecdotes, stories, and sayings into a story form, however loosely, complements language arts skills, and gives an appreciation for and sense of story. But perhaps more important, it shows children that they are worth the attention and interest of their teacher and classmates.

Family stories are a unique way for students to become familiar with relatives who are long since dead or whom they've never met. Martha grew up on a farm in a little town in Tennessee. Her mother came from a family of nine, so she was surrounded by aunts, uncles, and cousins. Her Uncle Henry died when she was six years old. Although she does have vague memories of him, she feels she has become reacquainted with Uncle Henry through the stories of her Aunt Frances. This is just one of the stories Frances told.

Why, Martha Jo, that Henry was a bushel of fun. The thing I remember most was how much he loved to eat. Nobody loved to eat like Henry. And when you've got nine kids sometimes you've got to kind of fight it out for the food. You see there was seven girls and two boys in our family and us girls always helped Mama do the cooking and baking. And Henry was the awfulest thing you ever seen about eatin' up things we'd cooked. We'd be baking some cornbread or some biscuits or something and he'd run into the kitchen and grab him a piece and high tail it out of there before we could say a word. And that would make us madder than a wet hen! Once Cynthy and Mildred baked three or four peach pies and set 'em out to cool. And Henry come into the kitchen and grabbed him a pie and a fork and went to running. Well, Cynthy lit out after him and he knew she was afraid of heights so he run all the way up to the attic and crawled out the window and got on the roof of the house. And all Cynthy and Mildred could do was stand outside and watch him sitting up there smiling and eating that whole pie. Of course, they told Mama and Poppy on him, and they was going to punish him but he got such a stomach ache—he moaned and groaned like a sick raccoon—so they decided that he had punished himself.

That Henry was such a practical joker. He loved playing tricks on people. You see all of us had jobs around the house. Well, me and Mildred—one of our jobs was to bring in the firewood. We had a big old stack of firewood out in the backyard. Well, every day I'd go out and get my pile and bring it in before suppertime.

But that Mildred—she'd keep puttin' it off and puttin' it off and 'fore you know it it'd be dark. Now I swear Mildred was scared of a mouse, so she'd start whining and saying, "Now Frances, I can't go out there by myself. You come with me." Or "Henry, I'm scared. Come help me git my stack of firewood."

Well, we all got sick and tired of that pretty quick and one day Henry made up his mind he's gonna break her of that. He told all of us kids to say we couldn't go—that we was busy or whatever. So it ended up that Mildred just had to go get that wood by herself. Then Henry went and got him a big old

Sarah, a seventh grader, discovers how her grandparents met during an interview with her grandmother.

white sheet and he put that thing over his head and went and hid behind that woodpile, and when he heard her a comin', he rose up from behind that big pile of wood and went to flappin' his arms and howling, "Woo! Woo!"

Well, that just about scared Mildred to death. She dropped what little wood she had and started to run, but she tripped and fell down and she's just laying there on the ground trying to get up but she couldn't, and she's trying to call for help but there was nothin' comin' out but this little "Help!"

And, of course, all us other kids was watching from the back door and just laughing and laughing. And I'll tell you one thing—even though Mildred finally realized it wasn't a real ghost, that it was just Henry—still from then on she always brought her stack of wood in before it got dark!

When you give examples of your own family or experience stories be sure to begin with commonplace topics to which your students can relate. As author Nancie Atwell comments in *In the Middle:*

I hope students will begin to engage in the important business of making sense of their ordinary, everyday worlds. I'm also hoping to dissuade them from a belief widely held among eighth graders that good writers are people who have had great experiences. All of us have heard students say "I don't know nothing. I've never done nothing." If I model as a topic my first view of the Acropolis by moonlight, I'm not going to inspire kids' confidence in the significance of their experiences. I do, in fact, write a lot about my dog and my childhood, subjects that have more to do with who I am and how I live than my week's tour of Athens. These are common experiences that to one degree or another are shared by all kids, and I want the stories I model to help students find their own—(*Atwell, 1987, p. 82*).

In addition to telling students your own family stories, an excellent way to kick off a family story unit is to read them a variety of stories from *A Celebration of American Family Folklore* edited by Steven J. Zeitlin and others. This book contains a selection of stories and photographs collected at the family folklore tent at the annual Smithsonian Folklife Festival in Washington, D.C. Each chapter includes a different category of story; for example, migrations, lost fortunes, courtships, or heroes. These stories will certainly trigger your students' memories.

We recently led a family stories residency at a high school. Faced with a classroom of reserved teenagers we told them a few of our own stories and then read them a couple of tales from the chapter in the book entitled "Supernatural Happenings." It wasn't long before students in the class were relating encounters they'd had with ghosts and other supernatural beings. Before we knew it the forty-five-minute class had flown by and we had their attention for the rest of the week.

We've included handouts at the end of this chapter that will get your students thinking about stories from their lives and will give them ideas on how to go about interviewing family members. As they gather stories from their relatives, or depend on their own memories, they begin to take great pride in what they've discovered. These stories are theirs and only they can tell them.

Most of the stories they bring to class will be in the form of short anecdotes. Let them share these stories in small groups and then, based on their preferences and the feedback of their listeners, choose one story to develop fully for telling. "Developing Your Story for Telling" at the end of the chapter will give them ideas for fleshing out their stories. It can be used as a handout for older students. For students younger than fifth graders you can use it as a lesson plan.

We feel it is best for students to write out a version of their stories. This will help immensely in the process of organizing the stories into coherent narrative form. If you already use the writing process approach in your class you can utilize the same techniques. Have students write out a rough draft and share it with a peer. Then they can rewrite their stories and, if need be, rewrite them again.

Once they write them down, they have the tendency to think that this is the only way the story can be told. To counter that idea, the best thing to do is to turn to Chapter 6, "Helping Children Learn Their Stories," and use many of the exercises given for learning a folk tale. Have the children outline their stories and work from the outline rather than the text. This will allow their stories to change and grow.

When students begin to tell their stories you can use the same exercises as in Chapter 7, "Helping Children Tell Their Stories," to improve their telling techniques. They can publish books[13] with their individual stories or compile a class collection of family stories into a magazine. You could do a bulletin board display with stories, using old photos and other appropriate materials. You might also want to have a family night when those who wish can share their stories with an audience of parents, grandparents, and other family members.

Some useful sources to help you get the project off the ground are:

Fletcher, William. *Recording Your Family History*. N.Y.: Dodd Mead, 1986.

Weitzman, David. *My Backyard History Book*. Boston: Little, Brown, 1973.

Wigginton, Eliot. *Foxfire*. Volumes 1–9. Garden City, N.Y.: Anchor, 1972–1986.

Zeitlin, Steven J., Amy J. Kotkin, and Holly Cutting Baker, eds. *A Celebration of American Family Folklore*. N.Y.: Pantheon, 1982.

Zimmerman, William. *Instant Oral Biographies*. N.Y.: Guarionex, 1981.

The articles listed below offer a variety of approaches for using family/experience stories in the classroom:

Gundlach, Susan. "Teaching Writing with Family Stories." *The National Storytelling Journal*. 3.4, 1986: 17–20.
Describes a writing project done with eighth graders. Students interviewed relatives and shaped the information they collected into story form.

Herman, Gail, and Claire Krause. "A Trunkful of Family Stories." *The National Storytelling Journal*. 4.3, 1987: 18–20.
Outlines a project done with a group of gifted and talented students in grades K–4. The emphasis in this case was on telling techniques rather than on writing.

---

[13] In more and more classrooms students are "publishing" their own books. These are stories they have written, illustrated, and bound. Often there is a library card in the back so that other students can take them out and read and enjoy them.

Stahl, Mark B. "Leaves from a Teacher's Notebook: Using Traditional Oral Stories in the English Classroom." *The English Journal*. October 1979: 33–36.

Discusses the value of using family stories as the basis for an exciting approach to teaching literature, writing, and language. Students respond enthusiastically because they personally value the stories. Explains how these stories can be used to improve students' understanding of what makes a story, the characteristics of oral language, the differences between written and oral language, and the importance of a good writing style. The focus is on middle and high school students.

HANDOUT: QUESTIONS TO HELP YOU REMEMBER STORIES
FROM YOUR OWN EXPERIENCE

What are the funniest things that have happened to you? _____

_____

_____

What was the most embarrassing thing that ever happened to you?

_____

_____

What was the most important event in your life so far? _____

_____

What is your favorite place or spot in the world? Why? _____

_____

What kinds of things have happened there? _____

_____

What happened on the day you were born? (Ask your parents.) __

_____

Are there other favorite stories your parents like to tell about you
that happened when you were too little to remember them? _____

_____

How did you get your name? _____

_____

Do you have any nicknames? How did you get them? _____

_____

What was the best gift you ever got? Why? _____

_____

Do you have any things which are really important to you because
they have a story behind them? What are they and what stories are
attached to them?

_____

_____

What happened on your first day of school? _____
_____

Were you ever lost? If so, what happened? _____
_____

Were you ever really scared by something? If so, what happened?
_____

Do you have any interesting stories about pets? _____
_____

Have you ever been on a vacation with your family? Did anything
interesting or funny happen? Describe your experiences. _____
_____

Have you even been to camp? If so, have any interesting things happened there or while you were camping with your family? _____
_____

_____

Did you ever play a practical joke on someone? What happened?
_____

Did someone ever play a practical joke on you? What happened?
_____

Are there things which have happened to you that make you sad to
think about them? Describe your experiences. _____
_____

_____

Are there any good stories based on dreams you have or things you
wish might happen? Describe them. _____
_____

HANDOUT: QUESTIONS YOU CAN ASK YOUR PARENTS, GRANDPARENTS, AUNTS, UNCLES, OR OTHER FAMILY MEMBERS

Every family has interesting stories to tell. Older family members especially love to tell stories of their younger days. To get them started, you can ask your relatives some of the same questions you asked yourself. In addition, you may want to ask them some of these questions. Remember that they are just suggestions to give you ideas of what to ask. You should come up with a list of questions which interest you most. Another good way to get your relatives telling stories is to have them take out old photographs. There are always interesting stories to be told about the people in the pictures.

It's a good idea to make a date with whomever you plan to interview. If you don't have access to a tape recorder take good notes and be sure to get all the details of any story in which you're particularly interested. If you tape the interview remember that it may be hard to find a particular story later. Taking brief notes as you go will make this process much easier.

When did you (or your ancestors) come to this country?

_____

_____

Why did they leave their homeland? _____

_____

_____

How was the journey made and where did they first settle?

_____

_____

What did they do for work? _____

_____

Do we have any interesting ancestors or relatives? Who? _____

_____

_____

Did anyone ever do anything really brave or interesting? What?

_____

_____

Where does our family name come from? _____

_____

What does it mean? _____

_____

What is its history? _____

_____

_____

What was your first school like? _____

_____

_____

Do you remember what happened the first day? _____

_____

_____

Any other memorable events? _____

_____

_____

Who are the teachers you remember? Tell me about them. _____

_____

_____

What was the worst trouble you ever got into? _____

_____

_____

What was the worst punishment you ever received? _____

_____

_____

What was the best/worst birthday you ever had? _____

_____

_____

_____

How did your family celebrate holidays such as Christmas or Hanukkah when you were little? _____

_____

_____

_____

How did you and Dad (Mom) meet? _____

_____

_____

How about Grandma and Grandpa? _____

_____

_____

How about Great-grandma and Great-grandpa? _____

_____

_____

Do you remember any weather disasters? What were they?

_____

_____

Were you ever caught in a storm? What happened? _____

_____

_____

_____

Did you ever play a practical joke on someone? Describe it.

_____

_____

Did someone ever play one on you? Describe it. _____

_____

_____

_____

Do you remember any good folk tales, legends, or ghost stories that
you heard when you were growing up? If so, would you tell it/them
to me? _____

_____

_____

_____

_____

Do you remember learning how to ride a bike or drive a car? Describe your experience. _____

_____

_____

_____

Do you remember when you first saw an airplane or rode on one for
the first time? Describe your experience. _____

_____

_____

_____

Were you ever afraid of the dark? Why? _____

_____

_____

What nightmares or dreams do you remember? Describe them.

_____

_____

Did anything really scary ever happen to you? What was it?

_____

_____

Did you have any toys that you still remember? Describe them.

_____

_____

Did you have a treehouse or secret hideout? Describe it. _____

_____

_____

_____

Do you remember having a favorite outfit when you were a kid?
Describe it. _____

_____

_____

When and where did you wear it? _____

_____

_____

How'd you get it? _____

_____

_____

Were you ever forced to wear clothes you didn't like? Describe them.

_____

_____

Did you have a TV in the house when you were growing up?

_____

_____

What were your favorite shows? _____

_____

_____

If you didn't have one, what did the family do for entertainment?

_____

_____

Do you remember when you first saw a TV? Describe your experience. _____

_____

_____

    In addition to these other questions, ask your grandparents if they remember any good stories about your father or mother when they were your age.

HANDOUT: DEVELOPING YOUR STORY FOR TELLING

Once you've decided on a story you must begin to flesh it out and eventually write it in story form. You should consider these story elements:

PLOT

Make a list of the events in the story as they happened. You will want to ask yourself: Are there any gaps or confusing parts in my story which I need to clarify or flesh out?

The best way to find out if your story line will be clear to others is to tell someone. You may start off with a simple one-liner story, such as Colleen Hutchings, a seventh grader from Piffard, New York, developed. She began with: "When I was little I threw a coin in the fountain at the shopping mall and fell in!" Her listeners asked questions such as: "How deep was the fountain? Were you in any danger of drowning? Exactly how old were you? How did you feel when you fell in? What did your mother do when she discovered what had happened?"

Colleen realized that her fall in the fountain triggered many different images among her listeners. Because she was the one to whom the incident had happened, she knew she was in no danger, but it was important that she transmit this information to everyone listening.

When telling a family story, it is important to make sure that everyone will see the action the way you do. So Colleen thought some more about her story and ended up telling it this way:

> When I was three years old my mom and her best friend took me with them to the shopping mall. We were standing by the fountain when my mom, who was busy talking to her friend, handed me a penny to throw in. When I leaned over to throw it in I FELL INTO THE FOUNTAIN! The water was only up to my knees so I wasn't scared. In fact, I had the opposite reaction. I saw all the coins and started gathering them up. All of a sudden my mother looked around and didn't see me, and so she started shouting "COLLEEN! COLLEEN!" When she realized what had happened she pulled me, soaking wet, from the fountain, and made me leave all the coins there. My mom says that for the longest time she would always steer clear of that fountain when we went to the mall.

Colleen didn't remember exactly how the incident had happened so she had to fill in the details from her imagination. This is called "poetic license." It may also be necessary to fill in details when a relative can't remember the fine points of a story.

SETTING

Use your five senses to describe the setting. Ask yourself: "How can I make the setting come alive for my listeners?"

We often tend to think that we have only eyes to use for describing our environment. Remember all of your senses: "What did I (or the main character) see? Hear? Smell? Taste? Feel?"

For example, if you were telling a story about your grandfather walking through a graveyard on a cold windy night you could ask yourself:

How would the wind have sounded? How would the cold have felt?

As he walked the snow crunched under his feet and the wind sounded like a pack of hungry wolves.

What might he have seen?

All around him, dark shadows were reflected on the white snow.

As a storyteller and writer you will find that looking at your story through your five senses will help you to fill in important and interesting details.

BEGINNING

The beginning of a story should introduce the reader to:

1. the main characters.

2. the time and place of the story.

3. the problem to be solved.

4. the conflict that is the essence of the story.

Ask yourself: How can I really grab my listeners' attention and draw them into the story right away?

Beginnings should be brief and to the point!

POINT OF VIEW

Ask yourself: Who should tell the story? Should I tell it in the first person as if it really happened to me?

Kim Krywe, an eighth grader from Leicester, New York, told a story about how her great-great-grandfather, Asa Noah Deal, had almost died during the Civil War. He had been saved by his best friend, George Wolfe, and she decided to tell the story from Wolfe's perspective.

> My name is George Wolfe, and I'd like to tell you about a time in my life where I felt like a real hero. It was in the Battle of Gettysburg during the Civil War, and I was one of many Union soldiers. We were all on top of Little Big Top looking down on the Confederates. My best friend was also a soldier. His name was Asa Noah Deal.
>
> We were going down, and the Confederates were coming up. The only shelter we had were big rocks. We kept running from one to the next. There was a lot of commotion, and by the end, many soldiers were wounded. There was a stream below that ran bright red with blood. When I got back to camp I realized Asa was not around. First I calmed myself down; then I went to the General to find out what had happened. He said in a gruff trying-to-be-gentle voice that there were many soldiers wounded, and that only the ones who were sure to live were supposed to be taken back to camp because first-aid supplies were limited. Asa was just one of the unlucky wounded or killed who couldn't be helped. Well, I wasn't just going to stand around and let my best friend who still might be alive just be left for dead. I was going to find him. And luckily enough, I did. I got him, and half-walked, half-pulled him all the way back to camp, and from there he was taken to the hospital.
>
> All of this took almost two days. I later learned that he had a big hole in his lung. And maggots had crawled in this hole and cleaned his wound. The doctors said that without the maggots, he would have died.

After that, he named his second son George after me. And that's why I'm proud to say that I was a hero at least once in my day.

The advantage to telling a story in the first person is that it draws the audience in right away because it sounds real. When using third person the teller is more distant from the tale, but the advantage is the allowance for certain observations and reflections that are not possible when speaking in the first person. You will need to decide which voice will be most appropriate for your story.

CHARACTERS

Ask yourself: How can I give all of my characters a distinct personality? How can I give my listeners an idea of what they're like without giving a long description?

Listeners must meet your main character. You already know your Aunt Tilly, but she is a stranger to your audience. You must bring her to life for them. This doesn't mean that you have to describe her in complete detail at the beginning of the story, but her character should come to life as the story moves along. This can be done by providing details you've chosen to weave into the story. By the end your listeners should feel as if they know Aunt Tilly themselves. You can:

1. Write down a list of the characters in your story.

2. For each of your characters list all the words you can think of to describe them.

3. For each of your characters jot down how you think they might have felt about the events in the story.

4. Write down any words or phrases you remember the character saying, or anything they might have said. Where or to whom would they have said this? How would they have sounded?

5. List any unusual objects or clothing that the person owned or wore.

Amie Pascuzzo, a fifth grade student from Retsof, New York, told this story. In her first paragraph she manages not only to convey a unique trait of her great grandfather to us but also she shows his relationship to her dad.

> My great-grandfather likes to paint things green. He painted the outside of his house green and the walls on the inside of his house green. He has this grandson—that's my father—and he used to always spoil my dad when he was a little boy.
>
> When my father was about five years old, my great-grandfather bought a brand new car. Everyone was surprised because it was light blue. He went inside to tell his wife about it. My dad was very mischievous and he decided to do some painting of his own. He found some green paint and painted the headlights green. When my great-grandpa came out he was very surprised to find a light blue car with green headlights!
>
> He took my dad and slapped his hands. My dad started to cry and said, "I don't understand! I don't understand! I thought you liked everything painted green." But he never did touch that paint again.

DIALOGUE

Ask yourself: How can I develop my characters by the use of dialogue?

In the preceding story it was much more effective when Amie said, "I don't understand! I don't understand! I thought you liked everything painted green," with expression and excitement than it would have been if she had simply said, "My dad started to cry and said he didn't understand because he thought his grandpa liked everything painted green." Dialogue can help listeners feel as if the event is taking place right before them. As the American writer Mark Twain once said: "Don't say the old lady screamed. Bring her on and let her scream."

Also, remember that you're not a reporter who must be concerned with repeating exactly what someone said. Instead you are trying to capture the flavor of what was said.

CONCLUSION

An ending should be satisfying. This doesn't mean that it has to be happy. It means that the ending must tie together all the parts of the plot in a satisfactory way. Even the shortest stories need to have a satisfying ending. Fifth grader Jenna Headley told her story this way:

> When my mom was sixteen she went to a skating rink. She saw this guy and she thought he was real cute, so she started chasing him around the rink. She wasn't looking where she was going and she crashed into a wall and broke her leg. The guy she had been chasing came over and helped her up and drove her to the hospital. That guy was my father and that's how my mom and dad met!

WRITE OUT A VERSION OF YOUR STORY

After considering the story elements listed above write out a version of your story. Read it to some of your classmates in order to get feedback. We have already discussed how important it is to be sure you have conveyed images clearly to your listeners. You'll be able to tell by the questions your listeners ask. When you feel your story is in a good form for telling, make an outline of it. Don't try to tell it in the exact words you've written. What you've written is *one* way to tell it, not the *only* way.

PRACTICE

Practice telling your story as many times as you can and you'll get better and better.

Each time you tell it, the story will be a little different. If you find that something you said didn't have the effect you had planned, you may want to change it or leave it out next time. A story is not complete until it is told. As you tell it, you will learn if you should have explained something better or if you went on a little too long. The more you tell it, the more confident you will become.

Have fun telling your story!

Chapter 10

How to Make Storytelling an Integral Part of Your Curriculum

Storytelling—both by you and by your students—can be an integral part of your curriculum. Stories fascinate children and serve to arouse their interest in and understanding of a subject. When you liven up your subject matter with stories, and encourage students to do the same by giving them the option of doing oral reports or telling stories instead of writing reports, you may be surprised by their enthusiasm.

> At the end of the year in social studies class, I let my sixth graders teach some lessons. This year India was our last country to study. I listed the topics on the board, *e.g.,* Indus River, Tigers, Taj Mahal. The children then chose and prepared their lessons. Although I had not taught any storytelling techniques this year, I had used stories in many of my lessons. It was a pleasant surprise when two girls included a story about elephants as an integral and natural part of their lesson!—(*Gibson*).

Bob Barton's and David Booth's *Stories in the Classroom* is an excellent source for helping teachers create and enrich the "storying" experience for every student. The book includes numerous story suggestions, as well as a host of interesting follow-up activities.

We suggest the following ideas for enlivening various subject areas.

LANGUAGE ARTS/ENGLISH

Listening to stories stimulates the imagination. With the appropriate follow-up, the enthusiasm of students can be directed toward creating their own stories. Here are some activities to get them started:

1. Have your students retell stories (as described in Chapter 2, "Retelling Stories").

2. Choose a character from a story you've told or read, and brainstorm a list of the character's qualities as a class activity. Then have the students, either individually or in small groups, make up a story where the character encounters new problems and adventures. As an example, read them Raymond Briggs' *Jim and the Beanstalk,* which recounts the later adventures of the Giant with a different boy. When you read or tell them *several* stories about the same character, such as Richard Chase's *The Jack Tales* or a few of the "Anansi the Spider"[14] stories, it will be even easier for them to make up their own stories. Students can eventually write their individual versions of the new stories and "publish" them.

3. Read/tell your class several variants of a folk tale in order to demonstrate how motifs recur again and again in folklore. Motifs are small bits of a plot which exist in more than one story. Examples of motifs include:

Mistreatment of a stepchild.

Fear test; for example, a person must sleep overnight in a haunted house.

Weak overcomes strong in a conflict.

Death portrayed as a person.

An adventure ensues after following an animal into a cave or hole in the ground which leads to a mysterious lower world.

In all versions of the classic tale of "The Sorcerer's Apprentice" there is the motif of someone setting magic in motion but not knowing how to stop it. You could read/tell your students several tales which include this motif, such as "The Master and His Pupil,"[15] "The Little Porridge Pot,"[16] and Tomie de Paola's *Strega Nona* (*see* "Works Cited" in Appendix A). Have your class brainstorm a list of the similarities among these stories. Then have them make up their own stories, including the same motif but with different characters and settings. You could even have them write a version incorporating names, places, and customs from your local area.

---

[14] A few suggested titles are Peggy Appiah. *Ananse the Spider: Tales from an Ashanti Village.* (N.Y.: Pantheon, 1966); Joyce C. Arkhurst. *The Adventures of Spider: West African Folk Tales.* (Boston: Little, Brown, 1964); Gerald McDermott. *Anansi the Spider: A Tale from the Ashanti.* (N.Y.: Holt, Rinehart and Winston, 1972); and Philip Sherlock. *Anansi the Spider Man, Jamaican Folk Tales.* (N.Y.: Crowell, 1954).

[15] In Joseph Jacobs. *English Fairy Tales.* (N.Y.: Dover, 1967).

[16] In Appendix B, "Twenty-five Stories for Children to Tell."

In order to get you started we've included two stories that re-volve around the motif of magic objects that are stolen from the owner by an innkeeper who is hosting the unsuspecting man for the night.

THE DONKEY, THE TABLE, AND THE STICK[17]

A lad named Jack was once so unhappy at home because of his father's ill-treatment that he made up his mind to run away and seek his fortune in the wide world.

He ran and he ran till he could run no longer, and then he ran right up against a little old woman who was gathering sticks. He was too much out of breath to beg pardon, but the woman was good-natured and she said he seemed to be a likely lad, so she would take him to be her servant and would pay him well. He agreed, for he was very hungry; and she brought him to her house in the wood where he served her for twelve months and a day. When the year had passed, she called him to her and said she had good wages for him. So she presented him with a donkey out of the stable; and he had but to pull Neddy's ears to make him begin at once to "hee–haw!" And when he brayed, there dropped from his mouth silver sixpences and half-crowns and golden guineas.

The lad was well pleased with the wage he had received, and away he rode till he reached an inn. There he ordered the best of everything, and when the innkeeper refused to serve him without being paid beforehand the boy went off to the stable, pulled the donkey's ears, and obtained his pocketful of money. The host had watched all this through a crack in the door, and when night came on he substituted a donkey of his own for the precious Neddy of the poor youth. So Jack without knowing that any change had been made, rode away next morning to his fa-ther's house.

Now, I must tell you that near his home dwelt a poor widow with an only daughter. The lad and the maiden were fast friends and true loves; but when Jack asked his father's leave to marry the girl: "Never till you have the money to keep her," was the reply. "I have that, father," said the lad, and going to the donkey he pulled its long ears. Well, he pulled and he pulled till one of them came off in his hands; but Neddy, though he "hee-hawed" and he "hee-hawed" let fall no half-crowns or guineas.

The father picked up a hayfork and beat his son out of the house. I promise you he ran. Ah! he ran and ran till he came bang against a door, and burst it open and there he was in a carpenter's shop.

---

[17] Adapted from Joseph Jacobs. "The Ass, the Table, and the Stick," from *English Fairy Tales*. (N.Y.: Dover, 1967), pp. 206–210.

"You're a likely lad," said the carpenter; "serve me for twelve months and a day and I will pay you well." So Jack agreed, and served the carpenter for a year and a day. "Now," said the master, "I will give you your wage," and he presented him with a table, telling him he had but to say: "Table, be covered," and at once it would be spread with lots to eat and drink.

Jack hitched the table on his back, and away he went with it till he came to the inn. "Well, host," shouted he, "my dinner to-day, and that of the best."

"Very sorry, but there is nothing in the house but ham and eggs."

"Ham and eggs for me!" exclaimed Jack. "I can do better than that.—Come, my table, be covered!"

At once the table was spread with turkey and sausages, roast mutton, potatoes, and greens. The innkeeper opened his eyes wide, but he said nothing.

That night he fetched down from his attic a table very like that of Jack, and exchanged the two. Jack, none the wiser, next morning hitched the worthless table on his back and carried it home. "Now, father, may I marry my lass?" he asked.

"Not unless you can keep her," replied the father.

"Look here!" exclaimed Jack. "Father, I have a table which does all my bidding."

"Let me see it," said the old man.

The lad set it in the middle of the room and bade it be covered; but all in vain, for the table remained bare. In a rage the father took the warming-pan down from the wall and warmed his son's back with it so that the boy fled howling from the house, and ran and ran till he came to a river and tumbled in. A man picked him out and bade him help him in making a bridge over the river; and how do you think he was doing it? Why, by casting a tree across; so Jack climbed up to the top of the tree and threw his weight on it, so that when the man rooted the tree up, Jack and the tree-head dropped on the farther bank.

"Thank you," said the man, "and now for what you have done I will pay you." So saying, he tore a branch from the tree and carved it up into a club with his knife. "There," exclaimed he, "take this stick, and when you say to it: 'Up stick and bang him,' it will knock any one down who angers you."

The lad was overjoyed to get this stick. So away he went with it to the inn, and as soon as the innkeeper appeared, Jack cried: "Up stick and bang him!" At these words the stick flew from his hand and battered the man until he begged Jack to make the stick stop. But Jack would not call it off till he had got back the stolen donkey and table. Then he galloped home on the donkey, with the table on his shoulders and the stick in his hand.

When Jack arrived his father was ready to drive him away

again until Jack showed his father the real magic gifts. He pulled the donkey's ears and golden coins spilled to the floor. He commanded the table: "Come, my table, be covered!" and a huge feast appeared.

"Now, father, may I marry my lass?" Jack did not have to use his stick to convince his father that he would now be wealthy enough to take care of the lass. And so it was that Jack and the maiden were married and they lived happily ever after.

THE LAD WHO WENT TO THE NORTH WIND [18]

Once upon a time there was an old widow who had one son. As she was old and weak, her son had to go up into the safe to get the cornmeal for cooking. But when he got outside the safe with the meal and was just going down the steps, there came the North Wind puffing and blowing. The North Wind caught the meal, and blew it away through the air.

Then the lad went back into the safe for more; but when he came out again on the steps the North Wind came again and carried off the meal with a puff! And more than that, he did so the third time. At this the lad got very angry. As he thought it unfair that the North Wind should behave so, he decided he'd just look him up and ask him to give back the meal.

So off he went. But the way was long and he walked and walked. At last he came to the North Wind's house.

"Good day!" said the lad. "I thank you for coming to see us yesterday."

"Good day!" answered the North Wind, and his voice was loud and gruff. "Thanks for coming to see me. What do you want?"

"Oh," answered the lad, "I only wished to ask you to be so good as to let me have back the meal you took from me on the safe steps. We haven't much to live on; and if you're to go snapping up the morsel we have, there'll be nothing for us to do but to starve."

"I haven't got your meal," said the North Wind. "But if you are in such need I'll give you a cloth which will get you everything you want. You have only to say, 'Cloth, spread yourself, and serve up all kinds of good dishes!' And the cloth will."

With this the lad was well content. But, as the way was so long he couldn't get home in one day, so he turned into an inn on the way. When they were going to sit down to supper he laid the cloth on a table which stood in the corner and said, "Cloth, spread yourself, and serve up all kinds of good dishes!"

[18] Adapted from Peter C. Asbjornsen and Jorgen E. Moe. "The Lad Who Went to the North Wind" from *Popular Tales from the Norse*, George W. Dasent, translator. (Edinburgh: David Douglass, 1888).

He had scarce said so before the cloth did as it was bid; and all who stood by thought it a fine thing, but most of all the landlord. So, when all were fast asleep at dead of night, the landlord took the lad's cloth and put another in its stead, just like the one the lad had got from the North Wind, but which couldn't so much as serve up a bit of dry bread.

When the lad awoke, he took his cloth and went off with it; and that day he got home to his mother.

"Mother," he said, "I've been to the North Wind's house, and a good fellow he is, for he gave me this cloth. When I say to it, 'Cloth, spread yourself, and serve up all kinds of good dishes!' I get any sort of food I please."

"All very true, I dare say," said his mother. "But seeing is believing, and I shan't believe it till I see it."

So the lad made haste, drew out a table, laid the cloth on it, and said, "Cloth, spread yourself, and serve up all kinds of good dishes!"

But not even a bit of dry bread did the cloth serve up.

"Well," said the lad, "there's no help for it but to go to the North Wind again." So away he went.

Late in the afternoon he came to where the North Wind lived.

"Good evening!" said the lad.

"Good evening!" said the North Wind.

"I want that meal of ours which you took," said the lad. "As for the cloth I got, it isn't worth a penny."

"I've got no meal," said the North Wind. "But here is a ram which coins nothing but golden ducats. You have only to say to it, 'Ram, ram, make money!' And it will."

So the lad thought this a fine thing. But, as it was too far to get home that day, he turned in for the night at the same inn where he had slept before.

Before he called for anything, he tried the truth of what the North Wind had said of the ram, and found it all right. When the landlord saw that, he thought it was a fabulous ram. So, when the lad had fallen asleep, he took another ram which couldn't coin golden ducats, and changed the two.

Next morning off went the lad. When he got home to his mother, he said, "After all, the North Wind is a jolly fellow, for now he has given me a ram which can coin golden ducats. I have only to say to it, 'Ram, ram, make money!'"

"All very true, I dare say," said his mother. "But I shan't believe any such stuff until I see the ducats made."

"Ram, ram, make money!" said the lad. But the ram made no money.

So the lad went back again to the North Wind and said the ram was worth nothing, and that he must have his rights for the meal.

"Well," said the North Wind, "I've nothing else to give you but that old stick in the corner yonder. But it's a stick of the kind that if you say, 'Stick, stick, lay on!' it lays on till you say, 'Stick, stick, now stop!'"

The lad took the stick. As the way was long he turned in this night at the same inn. By now the lad could pretty well guess how things stood as to the cloth and the ram. So he lay down at once on the bench and began to snore as if he were asleep.

Now the landlord, who easily saw that the stick must be worth something, hunted up one which looked just like it. When he heard the lad snore, he was going to change the two; but, just as the landlord was about to take the stick, the lad cried out, "Stick, stick, lay on!"

The stick began to beat the landlord till he jumped over chairs and tables and benches. He roared and yelled.

"Oh, my! Oh, my!" cried the landlord. "Bid the stick be still, else it will beat me to death! You shall have back both your cloth and your ram."

When the lad thought the landlord had got enough, he said, "Stick, stick, now stop!"

Then the lad took the cloth and put it into his pocket, and went home with his stick in his hand leading the ram by a cord round its horns.

The lad's mother was very happy when the cloth spread the good dishes on the table and when the ram coined golden ducats. And they were both very glad to have the stick which they knew would come in handy to keep away robbers.

Margaret Read MacDonald's *The Storyteller's Sourcebook* includes a motif index that lists stories according to similarity of motif. Another excellent source of ideas for using folk tales in the classroom is Bette Bosma's *Fairy Tales, Fables, Legends, and Myths: Using Folk Literature in Your Classroom*. It includes an entire chapter on "Learning to Write with Folk Literature."

4. Students will enjoy writing modern versions of classic children's stories.

Younger students will enjoy providing the story for Brinton Turkle's wordless *Deep in the Forest*, a topsy-turvy version of "Goldilocks and the Three Bears," in which a bear visits the home of a little girl and her parents. Older students will enjoy hearing James Thurber's "The Little Girl and the Wolf" from his *Fables for Our Times*. After reading it as an example, have students write their own versions of "Little Red Riding Hood." They could tell it from the wolf's point-of-view using the first person; they could change the setting of the story to a city; they could change the plot radically—

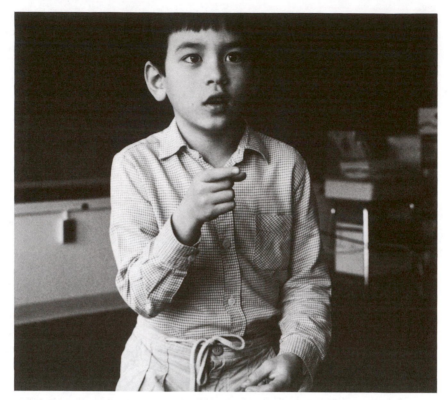

Karl creates an eerie mood while telling "Dark, Dark, Dark."

Little Red never liked her grandmother anyway, and so she and the wolf become a team. If they prefer, they could rewrite other classic stories (for example, Cinderella's stepsisters won't let her go to the "mall" instead of the "ball").

5. Have students form a *story circle*. The teacher begins a story with one sentence (or paragraph), such as: "One day I went out for a walk and all of a sudden I found myself lost in a deep, dark forest. . ." Each student continues the story around the circle by adding a sentence. It's a good idea to set a maximum time limit. To make it more interesting, try variations such as spinning a bottle to decide who tells next, or drawing names from a hat.

6. Give students two or three archetypal characters—an old man, an evil serpent, a wise queen, a foolish lad, a wizard—and have them tell the story of their adventures together. Or better yet, have students prepare cards with various character, setting, and problem ideas. Place the cards in boxes that are labeled *Character, Setting,*

and *Plot*. Then have students choose a card from each box and make up a story incorporating the various ideas.

7. When children give oral reports as part of a factual unit in the curriculum, they are often so concerned with content and accuracy that they give less priority to effective use of language. Assign a unit in which they don't have to worry about truth and accuracy, so that they can zero in on language skills. Let them give their imaginations free rein and tell the "tall tales" that are an important part of our American heritage. They can first study traditional American tall tales and then create their own.

   To get them started, give them sentences to complete. For example: "Paul Bunyan was almost as tall as _____." For more ideas consult Erma Prickett's "These Kids Tell Whoppers and Learn" (*Prickett, 1969*).

8. Tell part of a story, stop at the climax, and have students finish the story.

   You can also tell them stories which involve them in a decision. For example, older students will enjoy "The Cow-tail Switch,"[19] a West African story in which four skillful brothers each play an important part in resuscitating their father. One arranges his bones, the second covers the bones with flesh, the third adds blood, and the fourth gives him the power of speech. The listener must decide which brother deserves the reward of the cow-tail switch.

9. Have older students look for a newspaper article which interests them, and which might be used as the basis for a story.

10. We recommend *Storytelling Activities* by Norma Livo and Sandra Rietz, which includes several stories, as well as ideas for extending and reinforcing storytelling experiences (*see* "Works Cited" in Appendix A).

SCIENCE

1. All cultures have *pourquoi* or "why" stories. These are stories that were told when children asked questions such as: "Why do dogs and cats fight?" Or "Why does the sun shine during the day and the moon at night?" These "why" stories are helpful in arousing children's interest in a science class. The teacher could, for example, tell or read one or two stories used by other cultures to explain scientific phenomena,

[19] In Harold Courlander and George Herzog. *The Cow-tail Switch and Other West African Stories.* (N.Y.: Holt and Rinehart, 1947), pp. 5–12.

such as why the tides ebb and flow[20] or the changing of the seasons,[21] and then explain the scientific reason for these phenomena.

After hearing a few examples of these stories children could also be encouraged to make up their own "why" stories. According to Duncan Emrich's *The Hodgepodge Book,* Dora R. Elain, a third grade teacher, asked her students for their explanation of what causes thunder (*Emrich, 1972, pp. 175–176*). Their answers are the seeds of potential stories:

A. Thunder is a cart with a lot of sticks in it dropping out.

B. It's the angels bowling.

C. It's a giant walking across the Milky Way.

D. Thunder is a volcano in the sky erupting.

E. It's a potato bag with potatoes falling out.

F. Daddy says it's old man Joe moving his furniture.

We suggest the following as sources of stories and scientific explanations:

Climo, Shirley. *Someone Saw a Spider: Spider Facts and Folktales.* N.Y.: Crowell, 1985.

Devlin, Harry. *Harry Devlin's Tales of Thunder and Lightning.* N.Y.: Parent's Magazine, 1975.

2. People throughout the world have always been fascinated by celestial bodies and, as a result, folk literature abounds with stories about the moon, sun, and stars. If you are planning a unit on astronomy try beginning with one of these many tales, or have your students read a number of them. In glancing at MacDonald's *Storyteller's Sourcebook* we found an entire column of motifs listed under the single subject of "star." Some suggested collections are:

Gallant, Roy A. *The Constellations: How They Came to Be.* N.Y.: Four Winds, 1979.

Lurie, Alison. *The Heavenly Zoo: Legends and Tales of the Stars.* N.Y.: Farrar, Straus, and Giroux, 1979.

Mayo, Gretchen Will. *Star Tales: North American Indian Stories about the Stars.* N.Y.: Walker, 1987.

---

[20] *See* Joan Bowden. *Why the Tides Ebb and Flow* (Boston: Houghton Mifflin, 1979).
[21] *See* Gerald McDermott. *Daughter of the Earth: A Roman Myth* (N.Y.: Delacorte, 1984).

Monroe, Jean Guard, and Ray A. Williamson. *They Dance in the Sky*. Boston, MA: Houghton Mifflin, 1987.

You may want to have students create their own original stories to explain the existence of a constellation.

3. To make students aware on a more personal level of how much the world around them has changed in this century, and how it has affected older people in the community, have them interview older community members about advances in technology or changes in the environment. For example, they could ask: "Do you remember when your family first got a radio, television, or car?"

ECOLOGY

It is impossible for teachers to compete with the spectacular nature shows on television watched by many children nowadays. While telephoto lenses and time-lapse photography allow the viewer to witness a whole array of exotic wildlife and their behaviors they do not present a realistic view of nature. Children go on field trips and expect to see animals giving birth or fighting their enemies. Try telling a few stories to your class for an innovative approach to the subject matter. Although stories do not present a scientific view of nature, there are many folk tales that explain natural phenomena in an unusual way. This will arouse the interest of your students. On the first page of our "Bibliography of Suggested Stories for Students to Tell" (*see* Appendix A) you can see that Natalia Belting's book, *The Long-tailed Bear and Other Indian Legends* is full of stories that explain the oddities of nature. Check MacDonald's *Storyteller's Sourcebook* for more ideas.

Another excellent source is *Keepers of the Earth: Native American Stories and Environmental Activities for Children* by Michael J. Caduto and Joseph Bruchac. The book is a collection of Native American Indian stories and hands-on activities that promote understanding and appreciation of, empathy for, and responsible action toward the earth and its people.

SOCIAL STUDIES

By listening to the folk tales of various countries children begin to understand the many similarities and differences among cultures around the world. When studying a particular country take time to tell/read some folk tales that are told in that country. You will find MacDonald's *Storyteller's Sourcebook,*

Students' eager hands demonstrate how excitement about learning is easy to arouse when subjects are presented within the context of storytelling.

which includes an ethnic and geographic index, to be very useful for the purpose of locating stories.

HISTORY

1. The English novelist and poet Rudyard Kipling once said that if history was taught in the form of stories it would never be forgotten. And Marie Shedlock wrote in *The Art of the Storyteller:*

> I have always thought that the only way in which we could make either a history or literature lesson live, so as to take a real hold on the mind of the pupil at any age, would be that, instead of offering lists of events, crowded into the fictitious area of one reign, one should take a single event, say in one lesson out of five, and give it in the most splendid language and in the most dramatic manner . . . the stories [one chooses] must appeal so vividly to the imagination that they will light up the whole period of history

which we wish them to illustrate and keep it alive in the memory for all time"—(*Shedlock, 1951, pp. 152–153*).

2. Tell your students a story as if you were the President of the United States, the signer of a treaty, a soldier in the Revolutionary War, or a pilgrim newly arrived in this country. This will not only stimulate the students but also might help you to find new approaches to old material.

We were visiting Martha's family when her nephew, Michael, who at the time was a sophomore in high school, was complaining about his history class. The teacher had assigned each student to be an historical figure. As such, they were to prepare a eulogy for Napoleon's funeral that they would deliver orally. Michael, who was to be Beethoven, had discovered the link between the two: At one time Beethoven had been a great admirer of Napoleon and had originally dedicated his Third Symphony to him. He later tore up the dedication when Napoleon declared himself emperor.

Michael was distraught about the prospect of putting together a coherent eulogy and then delivering it in front of his classmates. When we asked what his teacher was like, he replied: "He's the best teacher I've ever had. You should see him in front of the class. He always participates when he gives us an assignment like this, and I'll bet his eulogy for Napoleon's funeral will be fantastic."

Clearly this teacher was a great role model and certainly had his students excited about history. Despite Michael's moaning he did a lot of research for the eulogy and said his delivery of it went really well.

Although most students will be terrified at the thought of doing an oral presentation in front of their classmates they will also admit that the rewards of doing a good job are far greater than for a written assignment, that they feel a great sense of gratification when they've finished.

3. In order to give your students a sense of history as actual events that happened to real people, have them interview their relatives or older members of the community about historical events such as the Great Depression, World War II, or where they were when John F. Kennedy was shot.

MATH

1. Word problems are really story problems.[22] Encourage your students to come up with their own creative stories to illustrate mathematical

---

[22]This idea was initially suggested to us by storyteller Jeannine Laverty.

problems. You could give each student a particular calculation that he or she must turn into a word problem to present to the rest of the class. Here's an example:

> There was once an absent-minded magician. Imagine what a problem this was! He was excellent at making rabbits and doves disappear, but, unfortunately, more often than not he could not bring them back. The magician never knew when he was going to open his closet door and find it filled with rabbits that he had been seeking for the past month. He asked all his magician friends for advice on improving his memory but nothing seemed to work.
>
> Now one day a traveling rabbit salesman, who had sold the magician many rabbits in the past, stopped at his house. On this particular day the magician bought 20 of the most beautiful white bunnies with long floppy ears. He had an important birthday party the next day, and knew everyone would be impressed by these new rabbits.
>
> That evening he practiced his most difficult tricks, including making a whole cageful of rabbits disappear. He placed half of the rabbits he had just bought in the cage. There were now _____ rabbits in the cage. He covered the cage with a sheet and then, after saying some magic words and waving his magic wand, he removed the sheet. Much to his dismay there were still 3 rabbits in the cage who had not disappeared. This had never happened before! He was so upset that he could not remember what had become of the rabbits that had disappeared. He searched all around his house but could not find them anywhere. At last he decided that the only thing that might possibly bring back his memory would be a good night's sleep. And, for once, the magician was right. When he pulled back the covers of his bed there, snuggled all together, were the _____ missing rabbits!

2. You can take tales you've told and extend them into basic math lessons. For example, if you read or tell Tomie de Paola's *Strega Nona* (in which Big Anthony disobeys Strega Nona and uses her magic pasta pot to make pasta for everyone in their town; then can't stop the pot, so the pasta covers the town; and, as punishment, Big Anthony has to eat up all the pasta) you can then ask the kids to pretend that the townspeople weighed all the pasta before Anthony ate it and found it weighed 500 pounds. Then have them do math problems such as: "If Big Anthony had eaten one-fourth of the pasta, how many pounds would be left?"

They can also make up problems of their own. One teacher mentioned to us that she asked her second graders: "What do you think the townspeople could have done with all that pasta if Big Anthony hadn't eaten it?" Her students came up with a recipe for pasta pudding, and

Students enjoy a chance to participate during a storytelling assembly by
Beauty & the Beast.

when they tried to figure out what they would mix it in, one boy said
they'd have to borrow a cement mixer!

Lynn Rubright, a storyteller and educational consultant, told
"Jack and the Beanstalk" and then asked students what they thought
the farmers should do about replacing all the equipment and belong-
ings that the giant had crushed when he fell from the beanstalk. They
figured out what was broken, and how much the total replacement
costs would be per farm (*Medina, 1986, p. 61*). The students were
having so much fun that they didn't realize they had just created their
own math lesson.*

ART

1. Children in today's society are so immersed in the images of the media—the images made by others—that it is often very difficult for

*The lesson is described in E. B. Medina's "Enhance Your Curriculum through Storytelling."

them to reach into their imaginations and see what is real for them. Yet simple storytelling calls up all kinds of vivid visual images that are raw material for art. You can have children draw, paint, or sculpt images they have created in their minds while listening to a story. Tell them that the images don't have to be realistic but can simply depict the mood or emotions of the story. Art teachers may be especially interested in the exercises for creating stories (*see* the first section, "Language Arts/English," of this chapter) since even those students who do not become totally absorbed when listening to someone tell a story will show more interest when they work to create their own stories.

Just as stories can effectively motivate children to produce original art, works of art can elicit creative, imaginative stories. Let students choose a work of art (from a selection of postcard or magazine reproductions or, if possible, works at a local museum) and encourage them to write stories based on the art. If some students choose the same work of art it's always interesting to compare and contrast the variety of stories written about it. Some suggested paintings to use are:

Marc Chagall. "I and the Village,"
Giorgio di Chirico. "The Melancholy and Mystery of a Street,"
Joan Miró. "Nursery Decoration,"
Pablo Picasso. "Girl Before a Mirror,"
Henri Rousseau. "The Sleeping Gypsy,"
Georges Seurat. "Sunday Afternoon on La Grande Jatte,"
Vincent Van Gogh. "Starry Night,"
Diego Velázquez. "The Maids of Honor."

2. Storytelling can also be used to foster an appreciation of works of art. Katherine Dunlap Cather wrote in *Educating by Storytelling*:

> [The child] must be taught to see that a Gainsborough is more beautiful than an advertising chromo, that a face by Raphael is the expression of an inspiration that is almost divine. Only through an association that gives pleasure will he come to see and appreciate, and here again storytelling can work wonders, because through it we can intensify a child's delight in a picture—(*Cather, 1920, pp. 97–98*).

Begin with the art form with which children are most familiar, that of the picture book. Tell them stories of the authors' lives. They will be very interested to know, for example, that Maurice Sendak's original plan was to write a book entitled *Where the Wild Horses Are*.

He eventually changed to *Where the Wild Things Are* because he found he couldn't draw horses well.[23]

Children will also enjoy Tomie de Paola's *The Art Lesson,* which is an autobiographical story showing how as a young boy he loved to draw pictures on anything, even his bedsheets, and knew he wanted to be an artist when he grew up.

You can eventually move to some of your favorite pieces of art. One way of arousing children's interest is to choose works that are based on a story. You could, for example, tell your students the story of Scheherazade, and then show them Henri Matisse's "The Thousand and One Nights." Or choose pieces that appeal to the children's interests and senses of color. Tell them about the artist's life and how he or she came to create the work. Children will be especially interested in the childhood of an artist.

Some useful articles that deal with the use of storytelling in the art class are:

Baumgartel, Marguerite, and Louise Lamb. "Listen, Imagine and Create." *School Arts,* September 1979: 40–41.
Includes a very short story about a visit to an unknown, imaginary planet. The objective of the story is to provoke creative artistic responses from elementary school children in an art education class.

Judson, Bay. "Once Upon a Time." *School Arts,* May 1983: 24–25.
Suggests ways in which storytelling can relate to visual images and help students to develop an appreciation of modern art. Questions about Matisse's "The Thousand and One Nights" are provided as an example.

MUSIC

The tradition of storytelling in many cultures appears to have its roots in music. Stories such as the ones we know about Robin Hood actually began as ballads sung by traveling minstrels. Folk songs depict the struggles and triumphs of the common people. For example, the songs of Woody Guthrie paint vivid images of the 1930s and 1940s in the United States.

There are many ballads useful for either telling or singing as part of the curriculum. A networking publication that gives many useful suggestions is *Folksong in the Classroom* (Laurence I. Seidman, Publisher, 140 Hill Park Avenue, Great Neck, N.Y. 11021. Subscription rates for individuals and institutions on request).

Other useful sources include:

[23] *See* Selma G. Lanes. *The Art of Maurice Sendak* (N.Y.: Abrams, 1980), p. 88.

Fox, Dan, and Claude Marks. *Go In and Out the Window: An Illustrated Songbook for Young People.* N.Y.: Metropolitan Museum of Art, 1987.

Jenkins, Ella. *The Ella Jenkins Song Book for Children.* Chester, N.Y.: Oak Publications (Box 572, Chester, N.Y. 10918), 1968.

Jones, Bessie, and Bess Lomax Hawkes. *Step It Down.* Athens, Ga.: University of Georgia Press (Terrell Hall, Athens, Georgia 30602), 1988.

Langstaff, John. *Hi! Ho! The Rattlin' Bog.* N.Y.: Harcourt, 1969.

Langstaff, John, and Nancy Langstaff. *Sally Go Round the Moon.* Cambridge, MA.: Revels Publications (Box 610, Cambridge, MA 02142), 1986.

Seeger, Ruth Crawford. *American Folksongs for Children.* N.Y.: Doubleday, 1948.

Chapter 11

Conclusion

For any teaching experience to be successful you must spark the interest of your students. Children, and adults, have been drawn by the power of storytelling for thousands of years. We urge you to awaken your students' sleeping imaginations by putting this ancient teaching tool to use in your classroom. As Kieran Egan has written:

> Imagination is not some desirable but dispensable frill, but . . . is the heart of any truly educational experience; it is not something split off from "the basics" or disciplined thought or rational inquiry, but it is the quality that can give them life and meaning; it is not something belonging properly to the arts, but it is central to all areas of the curriculum; it is not something to ornament our recreational hours, but is the hard pragmatic center of all effective human thinking . . . Stimulating the imagination is not an alternative educational activity to be argued for in competition with other claims; it is a prerequisite to making any activity educational—*(Egan, 1989, p. 458)*.

Storytelling will not only engage your students in the learning process in a new way but will keep teaching interesting for you, since stories can lend a fresh outlook to subjects that you may have been teaching and reteaching for a while. When you encourage your students to tell stories they will continually surprise you in ways you could never have predicted, as this sixth grade teacher found:

> Iman was from Iran. He had worked hard to lose his accent and to abandon his heritage at least during the school day. Even in social studies, when we talked of Middle East issues, he was quiet. Then he chose to tell "Hercules" for an assignment on Greek myths. Suddenly his accent returned. He sounded like a wise old Muslim storyteller when he began: "Now, children, I will tell you the tale of Hercules. He had to do not one, not five, not ten, but twelve labors, I tell you twelve labors. Hercules' first adventure took him . . ." The rhythms of Middle Eastern storytellers from ancient times came through his little twelve-year-old voice. The students liked his story so much they started telling other social studies classes to request he be released from my class to go on tour—*(Schwartz)*.

Nia's first attempt at telling her story in front of her class is a success.

During our ten years of telling stories we have made many return visits to schools. Even if a few years have passed, we are often approached by older students who still remember the stories we told earlier. And when children themselves do the telling it is bound to have even more lasting effects, as a fifth grade student remarked:

> My sister who is in high school came to the program to see me tell my story last night. She learned to tell a story when she was in fifth grade. When we got home she told me the story. Do you believe that she still remembered it?

Students take great pride in their stories. For some, they become old friends. They are treasures that they can take out of their pockets when the occasion arises, as one sixth grade boy commented:

> We always have skit night at Boy Scout camp—and last year I didn't do anything because I couldn't think of anything to do, but this year I'm going to tell my story.

If you need to convince other educators of the value of a storytelling unit give them copies of some of the numerous articles listed in the bibliography for this book, "Storytelling as an Educational Tool" in Appendix A. Or lend them a copy of this book and tell them to read Chapter 1. Initially, you may have to do some lobbying, since few administrators will recognize the educational value of storytelling until they can witness the results and see how much enthusiasm and interest is generated among students.

Good luck in your storytelling ventures. We'd love to hear about your experiences. And if you haven't yet told your first story, take this advice from a second grader:

I love to tell storys.
It is so easy. Hears how to.
Pick a story. Read it three
times. Then tell it
to someone with oat
the book. It is scary
at first and then you get
youst to it. You shud
try it. Its fun!!

Appendix A

Bibliographies

WORKS CITED

Atwell, Nancie. *In the Middle: Writing, Reading, and Learning with Adolescents*. Portsmouth, N.H.: Heinemann, 1987.

*Babcock, Sally Anne. Third Grade Teacher, Norwich, N.Y.

Barton, Bob, and David Booth. *Stories in the Classroom: Storytelling, Reading Aloud and Roleplaying with Children*. Markham, Ontario: Pembroke, 1990.

Belting, Natalia M. *The Long-tailed Bear and Other Indian Legends*. N.Y.: Bobbs-Merrill, 1961.

Bettelheim, Bruno. *The Uses of Enchantment: The Meaning and Importance of Fairy Tales*. N.Y.: Vintage, 1977.

Bosma, Bette. *Fairy Tales, Fables, Legends, and Myths: Using Folk Literature in Your Classroom*. N.Y.: Teacher's College Press, 1986.

Briggs, Raymond. *Jim and the Beanstalk*. N.Y.: Coward, McCann and Geoghegan, 1970.

Brown, Hazel, and Brian Cambourne. *Read and Retell: A Strategy for the Whole-Language/Natural Learning Classroom*. Portsmouth, N.H.: Heinemann, 1990.

Caduto, Michael J., and Joseph Bruchac. *Keepers of the Earth: Native American Stories and Environmental Activities for Children*. Golden, CO: Fulcrum, 1988.

Calkins, Lucy McCormick. *The Art of Teaching Writing*. Portsmouth, N.H.: Heinemann, 1986.

Campbell, Joseph. *The Power of Myth*. N.Y.: Doubleday, 1988.

Cather, Katherine Dunlap. *Educating by Storytelling*. N.Y.: World Book, 1920.

*Asterisks indicate those who contributed personal correspondence about their experiences teaching children to tell stories.

Chase, Richard. *Grandfather Tales*. Cambridge, MA.: Houghton Mifflin, 1948.

Cohen, Dorothy H. "The Effect of Literature on Vocabulary and Reading Achievement." *Elementary English,* February 1968: 209–213, 217.

Courlander, Harold. *The Cow-tail Switch and Other West African Stories*. N.Y.: Holt, Rinehart and Winston, 1947.

DePaola, Tomie. *The Art Lesson*. N.Y.: Putnam, 1989.

———. *Strega Nona*. Englewood Cliffs, N.J.: Prentice-Hall, 1975.

Egan, Kieran. "Memory, Imagination, and Learning: Connected by the Story." *Phi Delta Kappan*. February 1989: 455-459.

———. *Teaching as Story Telling: An Alternative Approach to Teaching and Curriculum in the Elementary School*. Chicago, Il.: The University of Chicago Press, 1986.

Emrich, Duncan. *The Hodgepodge Book*. N.Y.: Four Winds, 1972.

*Forest, Heather. Storyteller, Huntington, N.Y.

*Geisler, Harlynne. Storyteller, San Diego, CA.

*Gibson, Sharon. Sixth Grade Teacher, Bartlesville, OK.

*Gohl, Mary Jane. Third Grade Teacher. Norwich, N.Y.

Goodman, Kenneth S. *What's Whole in Whole Language*. Richmond Hill, Ontario: Scholastic, 1986.

*Hodges, Lois Foight. Children's Librarian, Schenectady, N.Y.

*Howard, Don. Third Grade Teacher, Oak Park, IL.

Jennings, Tim. "Storytelling: A Nonliterate Approach to Teaching Reading." *Learning*. April/May 1981: 49-52.

Kafka, Franz. *Selected Short Stories of Franz Kafka*. Prague: Heinr. Mercy Sohn, 1936.

*Kaminsky, Marty. Third Grade Teacher, Ithaca, N.Y.

Kipling, Rudyard. *Just So Stories*. N.Y.: Doubleday, 1909.

Leach, Maria. *The Thing at the Foot of the Bed and Other Scary Tales*. N.Y.: World, 1959.

Lester, Julius. *More Tales of Uncle Remus: Further Adventures of Brer Rabbit, His Friends, Enemies & Others*. N.Y.: Dial, 1988.

————. *The Tales of Uncle Remus*. N.Y.: Dial, 1987.

Livo, Norma J., and Sandra A. Rietz. *Storytelling Activities*. Littleton, CO: Libraries Un-limited, 1987. (To order write: P.O. Box 263, Littleton, CO 80160-0263).

•Locke, June. Elementary School Librarian, Enfield, N.Y.

MacDonald, Margaret Read. *The Storyteller's Sourcebook: A Subject, Title, and Motif Index to Folklore Collections for Children*. Detroit, MI.: Neal-Schuman, 1982.

————. *Twenty Tellable Tales: Audience Participation Folktales for the Beginning Storyteller*. N.Y.: Wilson, 1986.

————. *When the Lights Go Out: Twenty Scary Tales to Tell*. N.Y.: Wilson, 1988.

Maguire, Jack. *Creative Storytelling: Choosing, Inventing, and Sharing Tales for Children*. N.Y.: McGraw-Hill, 1985.

Marshall, James. *Tons of Fun*. Boston, MA.: Houghton Mifflin, 1980.

•McClear, Mary-Eileen. Storyteller, Baden, Ontario, Canada.

Medina, Elizabeth Brewster. "Enhance Your Curriculum through Storytelling." *Learning*. October 1986: 58-61.

•Moore, Joan. Reading Specialist, Smithtown, N.Y.

Morrow, Lesley Mandel. "Retelling Stories: A Strategy for Improving Young Children's Comprehension, Concept of Story Structure, and Oral Language Complexity." *The Elementary School Journal*. May 1985: 647-661.

Nessel, Denise D. "Storytelling in the Reading Program." *The Reading Teacher*. January 1985: 378-381.

Nixon, Joan Lowery. *Beats Me Claude*. N.Y.: Viking, 1986.

Padgett, Byron. "The Care and Feeding of a Child's Imagination." *Ms*. May 1976: 60-63 ff.

•Parent, Michael. Storyteller, Charlottesville, VA.

Prickett, Erma. "These Kids Tell Whoppers and Learn." *Grade Teacher*. September 1969: 130-134.

Reed, Barbara. "Storytelling: What It Can Teach." *School Library Journal*. October 1987: 35-39.

Rosen, Betty. *And None of It Was Nonsense: The Power of Storytelling in School*. Portsmouth, N.H.: Heinemann, 1988.

Rosen, Harold. "The Importance of Story." *Language Arts*. March 1986: 226-237.

Rubinstein, Robert E. "Student Storytelling: As Easy as 1-2-3-4." *Teacher.,* March 1973: 34-36.

Russell, William F. *Classic Myths to Read Aloud*. N.Y.: Crown, 1989.

Sandburg, Carl. *Rootabaga Stories*. N.Y.: Harcourt, Brace, 1922.

Schimmel, Nancy. *Just Enough to Make a Story: A Sourcebook for Storytelling*. Berkeley, CA: Sister's Choice, 1982.

*———. Storyteller, Berkeley, CA.

*Schwartz, Marni. Teacher and Storyteller, Schenectady, N.Y.

Shannon, George. "Storytelling and the Schools." *The English Journal*. May 1979: 50–51.

Shedlock, Marie. *The Art of the Storyteller*. N.Y.: Dover, 1951.

Smith, Frank. *Understanding Reading*. Hillsdale, N.J.: Erlbaum, 1988.

*Stallings, Fran. Storyteller, Bartlesville, OK.

———. "The Web of Silence: Storytelling's Power to Hypnotize." *The National Storytelling Journal* 5.2, 1988: 6-19.

Thurber, James. *Fables for Our Times*. N.Y.: Harper, 1940.

Trelease, Jim. *The Read-Aloud Handbook*. N.Y.: Penguin, 1982.

Turkle, Brinton. *Deep in the Forest*. N.Y.: Dutton, 1976.

U.S. Department of Education. *What Works: Research about Teaching and Learning*. Washington, D.C.: Department of Education, 1986.

Wallechinsky, David, and Irving Wallace. *The People's Almanac Presents the Book of Lists*. N.Y.: Morrow, 1977.

*Wasiewicz, Ann. Elementary School Librarian, Elbridge, N.Y.

Wells, Gordon. *The Meaning Makers: Children Learning Language and Using Language to Learn*. Portsmouth, N.H.: Heinemann, 1986.

*Wood, Sylvia. Second Grade Teacher, Bartlesville, OK.

Zeitlin, Steven J., Amy J. Kotkin, and Holly Cutting Baker, eds. *A Celebration of American Family Folklore*. N.Y.: Pantheon, 1982.

GENERAL WORKS ON STORYTELLING

Baker, Augusta, and Ellin Greene. *Storytelling: Art and Technique.* N.Y.: Bowker, 1987.

*Barton, Bob. *Tell Me Another: Storytelling and Reading Aloud at Home, at School and in the Community.* Markham, Ontario: Pembroke (distributed by Heinemann), 1986.

*————, and David Booth. *Stories in the Classroom: Storytelling, Reading Aloud and Roleplaying with Children.* Markham, Ontario: Pembroke, 1990.

Bauer, Caroline Feller. *Handbook for Storytellers.* Chicago, IL.: American Library Association, 1977.

Bettelheim, Bruno. *The Uses of Enchantment: The Meaning and Importance of Fairy Tales.* N.Y.: Vintage, 1977.

Breneman, Lucille, and Bren Breneman. *Once Upon a Time: A Storytelling Handbook.* Chicago, IL.: Nelson-Hall, 1983.

Greene, Ellin, and George Shannon. *Storytelling: A Selected Annotated Bibliography.* N.Y.: Garland, 1986.

*Livo, Norma J., and Sandra A. Rietz. *Storytelling Activities.* Littleton, CO: Libraries Unlimited, 1987. (To order write: P.O. Box 263, Littleton, CO 80160-0263).

————. *Storytelling: Process & Practice.* Littleton, CO: Libraries Unlimited, 1986.

*Maguire, Jack. *Creative Storytelling: Choosing, Inventing, and Sharing Tales for Children.* N.Y.: McGraw-Hill, 1985.

Pellowski, Anne. *The World of Storytelling.* N.Y.: Bowker, 1977.

Ross, Ramon. *Storyteller.* Columbus, OH.: Merrill, 1980.

Sawyer, Ruth. *The Way of the Storyteller.* N.Y.: Viking, 1942.

*Schimmel, Nancy. *Just Enough to Make a Story: A Sourcebook for Storytelling.* Berkeley, CA: Sister's Choice, 1982. (Available by mail from: Sister's Choice Press, 1450 Sixth Street, Berkeley, CA 94710)

Shedlock, Marie. *The Art of the Storyteller.* N.Y.: Dover, 1951.

Yolen, Jane. *Touch Magic: Fantasy, Faerie and Folklore in the Literature of Childhood.* N.Y.: Philomel, 1981.

Ziskind, Sylvia. *Telling Stories to Children.* N.Y.: Wilson, 1976.

*Although all of these sources are excellent, we have starred the five books we think would be most useful for teachers.

A useful tool to help you find stories on a specific subject or theme is:

MacDonald, Margaret Read. *The Storyteller's Sourcebook: A Subject, Title, and Motif Index to Folklore Collections for Children.* Detroit, MI.: Neal-Schuman, 1982.

STORYTELLING AS AN EDUCATIONAL TOOL*

Davis, Donald D. "Storytelling and Comprehension Skills: A Classroom Experiment." *The Yarnspinner* (newsletter of the National Association for the Preservation and Perpetuation of Storytelling). December 1982: 1-2.

Egan, Kieran. "Memory, Imagination, and Learning: Connected by the Story." *Phi Delta Kappan.* February 1989: 455-459.

Denman, Gregory A. *When You've Made It Your Own: Teaching Poetry to Young People.* Portsmouth, N.H.: Heinemann, 1988.
A professional storyteller discusses how children learn to love poetry through the art of storytelling. There are lots of activities and lists of poets and poems.

Farnsworth, Kathryn. "Storytelling in the Classroom—Not an Impossible Dream." *Language Arts.* February 1981: 162-167.

Frick, Hollee. "The Value of Sharing Stories Orally with Middle Grade Students." *Journal of Reading.* January 1986: 300-303.

Jennings, Tim. "Storytelling: A Nonliterate Approach to Teaching Reading." *Learning.* April/May 1981: 49-52.

Kingore, Bertha. "Storytelling: A Bridge from the University to the Elementary School to the Home." *Language Arts.* January 1982: 28-32.
As an Assistant Professor at Hardin Simmons University Kingore teaches a group of education students to tell stories. This troupe of tellers then goes to local elementary schools to share their stories, and encourages children to try learning a story themselves.

Koepke, Mary. "Telling Tales in School: A Revival of the Oral Tradition in the Nation's Classrooms." *Teacher.* February 1990: 30-33.

Medina, Elizabeth Brewster. "Enhance Your Curriculum through Storytelling." *Learning.* October 1986: 58-61.

Millstone, David H. "Homer's Odyssey: An Elementary Passion." *The Classical Outlook* 65.2. 1987-1988: 53-57.
This elementary school teacher describes a three-month storytelling collaboration between first and fifth graders which centered on their study of *The Odyssey.* Each

---

*This is a *selective* list of the most useful articles and books dealing with storytelling and education. We have included annotations when the title did not seem self-explanatory.

grade listened to storytellers relating different parts of the epic, and then students paired up (one fifth grader with one first grader) and retold the part they had heard. Millstone found that the project not only helped the children to absorb a classic work of literature thoroughly but also created strong friendships across grade levels.

Morgan, John, and Mario Rinvolucri. *Once Upon a Time: Using Stories in the Language Classroom.* London: Cambridge University Press, 1983.

Morrow, Lesley Mandel. "Retelling Stories: A Strategy for Improving Young Children's Comprehension, Concept of Story Structure, and Oral Language Complexity." *The Elementary School Journal.* May 1985: 647-661.

Nelson, Olga. "Storytelling: Language Experience for Meaning Making." *The Reading Teacher.* February 1989: 386-390.

Nessel, Denise D. "Storytelling in the Reading Program." *The Reading Teacher.* January 1985: 378-381.

Nietzke, Doug. "The Ancient New Method." *The Clearing House.* May 1988: 419-421.
A college English professor relates how he has learned to value stories as an integral part of his teaching. Includes a story which would be useful for history teachers at any level to explain the difference between primary and secondary sources.

Prickett, Erma. "These Kids Tell Whoppers and Learn." *Grade Teacher.* September 1969: 130-134.
A librarian describes a project she did with fifth and sixth graders centered on "tall tales." After reading the students numerous tall tales and discussing story structure, similes, and metaphors, the children created their own tall tales.

Reed, Barbara. "Storytelling: What It Can Teach." *School Library Journal.* October 1987: 35-39.

Rosen, Betty. *And None of It Was Nonsense: The Power of Storytelling in School.* Portsmouth, N.H.: Heinemann, 1988.

Rosen, Harold. "The Importance of Story." *Language Arts.* March 1986: 226-237.

Rubinstein, Robert E. "The Next Generation." *The Yarnspinner* (newsletter of the National Association for the Preservation and Perpetuation of Storytelling). December 1981: 1-2.
Describes the Roosevelt Troupe of Storytellers, a group of middle school students who take an initial course with Rubinstein and then tour local elementary schools.

————. "Steps to Selling that Storytelling Class." *The National Storytelling Journal* 5.2. 1988:21.
Tips on convincing administrators that storytelling goes far beyond entertainment.

————. "Student Storytelling: As Easy as 1-2-3-4." *Teacher.* March 1973: 34-36.

Schwartz, Marni. "Connecting to Language through Story." *Language Arts.* October 1987: 603-610.

———. "Storytelling: A Way to Look Deeper." *English Journal.* January 1989: 42-46. A middle school English teacher describes the impact of storytelling in her classroom.

———. "Storytelling in High School? Honestly." *Vital Signs.* James Collins, ed. Portsmouth, N.H.: Heinemann, 1989.

Shannon, George. "Storytelling and the Schools." *The English Journal.* May 1979: 50–51. A professional storyteller discusses why he feels storytelling deserves a valued place in the classroom.

"Storytelling and Education." Special Issue of *Parabola.* November 1979.

"Storytelling in Education." Special Issue of *The National Storytelling Journal* 3.4. 1986.

STORYTELLING ON VIDEO- AND AUDIOCASSETTE

Although video- or audiocassettes can never capture the full impact of a live performance by a storyteller they can introduce your students to a wide range of styles and traditions of storytelling. If you expose students to a number of storytellers chances are each student will be inspired by or be able to identify with at least one teller. They will certainly become aware that there are many ways to tell a story.

Check your school and public libraries for recordings. In some areas, for example, videos may be owned by a regional library system and may be available through interlibrary loan. We have compiled a selected list of recordings that have received good reviews in *The National Storytelling Journal.* When it was available we included the recommended age level for listeners. Some of these recordings are available from: The National Association for the Preservation and Perpetuation of Storytelling (NAPPS), P.O. Box 309, Jonesborough, Tennessee 37659. NAPPS will send you a free copy of *The National Storytelling Catalog* (includes fifty to sixty items) as well as a free up-to-date listing of other storytelling resources available. This list gives information on how to order items directly from the artist or distributor.

CASSETTE RECORDINGS/ALBUMS

Beauty & the Beast Storytellers. (Not in NAPPS catalog. For information write P.O. Box 6624, Ithaca, N.Y. 14851.) Our recordings include an audiocassette, *Tales of Wonder, Magic, Mystery and Humor from Around the World,* and a videotape in the *Tell Me a Story* series.

Davis, Donald. Born in the Southern Appalachian Mountains, Davis grew up hearing and repeating the tall tales and traditional stories of his Welsh and Scottish ancestors. *Traditional Tales for Children* and *More than a Beanstalk* are two of his many recordings for children.

Folktellers, The. These are two storytelling cousins from Asheville, North Carolina, whose repertoire features a colorful blend of humor, traditional mountain tales, and contemporary stories. Their recordings include *Tales to Grow On* for younger children; *White Horses and Whippoorwills* for junior high students and older; and *Chillers,* which includes "Mary Culhane," "How to Turn into a Witch," "Mr. Fox," and others.

Forest, Heather. Forest presents world folk tales in a minstrel style, blending movement, original song, guitar, poetry, and prose. Her recordings include *Songspinner: Folktales and Fables Sung and Told, Tales of Womenfolk* (all ages), and *Sing Me a Story* (preschool to elementary).

Holt, David. Holt performs music and stories he has collected throughout the Southern mountains, weaving music into his stories with banjo, guitar, hammered dulcimer, harmonica, and spoons. His recordings include *The Hairy Man and Other Wild Tales* and *Tailybone,* in which he tells "strange tales for the strong hearted, augmented by haunting music."

Keillor, Garrison. (Not in NAPPS catalog. Recordings available from the *Wireless* catalogue, Minnesota Public Radio, 274 Fillmore Avenue East, St. Paul, MN 55107.) The creator and star of the radio series, "A Prairie Home Companion," Keillor is America's best-known storyteller. *News from Lake Wobegon* is a collection of four cassettes including some of his best monologues. He can presently be heard on "American Radio Show of the Air" on public radio stations throughout the U.S.

Lieberman, Syd. Lieberman offers a good example of how to create stories from one's own experience. *A Winner and Other Stories* includes humorous tales for both teens and adults. *Joseph the Tailor and Other Jewish Tales* includes twelve stories adapted from folk and biblical material.

Martin, Rafe. *The Boy Who Loved Mammoths and Other Tales* includes energetic tellings of Native American tales, the original title story, and "The Three Little Pigs" (for elementary school children).

McGill Alice. McGill's *Flying Africans* includes a broad repertoire of stories drawn from African, Afro-American, and family sources.

Munsch, Robert. (Not in NAPPS catalogue. Recordings available from Kids Records, Box 670, Station A, Toronto, Ontario, Canada M5W 1G2.) This Canadian author/storyteller is known for his rollicking original tales. His recordings—*Robert Munsch: Favorite Stories, Love You Forever,* and *Murmel, Murmel*—include a live, appreciative audience that often joins in (for elementary school children).

NAPPS. The "National Association for the Preservation and Perpetuation of Storytelling" has issued a few collections including *Homespun Tales,* "country-flavored" tales told by Donald Davis, Jackie Torrence, The Folktellers, Doc McConnell, Elizabeth Ellis, and Kathryn Windham (for all ages); *Graveyard Tales,* designated a "Notable Recording" by the American Library Association, includes six haunting stories of the supernatural told with the chill of a live performance during the National Storytelling Festival (available both as album and cassette).

O'Callahan, Jay. Both a story maker and storyteller O'Callahan performs the stories he has woven from a measured blend of fact and fantasy. He has received both national and international acclaim for the power and integrity of his material and his performance. *Raspberries, Little Heroes, The Strait of Magellan,* and *The Little Dragon & Other Stories* are just a few of his many recordings.

Parent, Michael. A former high school English teacher Parent is a dynamic performer who tells both original and traditional stories. His recordings include *Tails and Childhood* and *Sundays at Grandma's.*

Rubright, Lynn. A major force in creating storytelling and education programs Rubright has recorded *Storytelling Teaching Tape,* which combines stories and suggestions for the use of storytelling in the classroom. Other recordings include *Lynn Rubright Tells Mike Fink Tall Tales* and *Rabbit's Tale and Other Native American Myths and Legends.*

Simms, Laura. Simms performs unusual and often powerful world tales. *Just Right for Kids, Stories: Old as the World, Fresh as the Rain,* and *There's a Horse in My Pocket* are among her recordings (for elementary school children).

Torrence, Jackie. One of America's best-loved storytellers "The Story Lady" tells stories from the Black American tradition. This internationally renowned teller has numerous recordings including *The Story Lady, Brer Rabbit Stories, Jack Tales Volumes 1 and 2, Legends from the Black Tradition,* and *Tales for Scary Times.*

VIDEOCASSETTES*

The American Storytelling Series. Eight videos feature stories told by twenty different storytellers. ¹/₂″ VHS.

Family Circle Presents Storyland Theater. A four-volume set that includes tales told by Rafe Martin, Laura Simms, and Jay O'Callahan, ¹/₂″ VHS.

Tell Me a Story. A collection of eight videos for children. Tellers include Nancy Schimmel, Chuck Larkin, Michael "Badhair" Williams, and Beauty & the Beast Storytellers. ¹/₂″ VHS.

*We know of only three series of storytelling videotapes. These come in a wide cost range.

Other videotapes include:

By Word of Mouth. An hour-long video documentary of the 10th National Storytelling Festival in 1982. It includes tellings by twenty-three nationally known storytellers. 1/2″ and 3/4″ VHS.

Jay O'Callahan. *Master Class in Storytelling* won first prize for teacher education at the 1985 National Educational Film Festival, and was designed as a focal activity for a storytelling workshop (VHS and BETA); and *Orange Cheeks, Herman & Marguerite,* and *Six Stories about Little Heroes,* available in 1/2″ and 3/4″ VHS.

SOURCES OF STORIES FOR TEACHERS TO TELL OR READ ALOUD

Two very useful bibliographies of stories good for telling are:

Cathon, Laura E., *et al. Stories to Tell to Children.* Pittsburgh, PA. University of Pittsburgh Press, 1974.

Iarusso, Marilyn Berg. *Stories: A List of Stories to Tell and to Read Aloud.* N.Y.: The New York Public Library, 1977.

STORY COLLECTIONS—FOLK TALES AND AUTHORED TALES

Arnott, Kathleen. *African Myths and Legends.* N.Y.: Henry Walck, 1963.

Babbitt, Natalie. *The Devil's Other Storybook.* N.Y.: Farrar, Straus and Giroux, 1987.

———. *The Devil's Storybook.* N.Y.: Bantam, 1977.

Bierhorst, John. *The Naked Bear: Folktales of the Iroquois.* N.Y.: Morrow, 1987.

———. *The Whistling Skeleton: American Indian Tales of the Supernatural.* N.Y.: Four Winds, 1982.

Bruchac, Joseph. *Iroquois Stories.* Trumansburg, N.Y.: Crossing, 1985.

———. *Stone Giants and Flying Heads: Adventure Stories of the Iroquois.* Trumansburg, N.Y.: Crossing, 1979.

———. *Turkey Brother and Other Tales: Iroquois Folk Stories.* Trumansburg, N.Y.: Crossing, 1975.

Buck, Pearl S. *Fairy Tales of the Orient.* N.Y.: Simon and Schuster, 1965.

Caduto, Michael J., and Joseph Bruchac. *Keepers of the Earth: Native American Stories and Environmental Activities for Children*. Golden, CO.: Fulcrum, 1988.

Chase, Richard. *Grandfather Tales*. Cambridge, MA.: Houghton Mifflin, 1948.

————. *The Jack Tales*. Cambridge, MA.: Houghton Mifflin, 1943.

Clarkson, Atelia. *World Folktales*. N.Y.: Scribner, 1980.

Cole, Joanna. *Best-loved Folk-Tales of the World*. Garden City, N.Y.: Doubleday, 1983.

Courlander, Harold, and George Herzog. *The Cow-tail Switch and Other West African Stories*. N.Y.: Holt, Rinehart and Winston, 1947.

———— and Wolf Leslau. *The Fire on the Mountain and Other Ethiopian Stories*. N.Y.: Henry Holt, 1950.

————. *People of the Short Blue Corn: Tales and Legends of the Hopi Indians*. N.Y.: Harcourt Brace Jovanovich, 1970.

Crossley-Holland, Kevin. *British Folk Tales: New Versions*. N.Y.: Orchard, 1987.

Curry, Jane Louise. *Back in the Beforetime: Tales of the California Indians*. N.Y.: Margaret K. McElderry, 1987.

Dewitt, Dorothy. *The Talking Stone: An Anthology of Native American Tales and Legends*. N.Y.: Greenwillow, 1979.

Erdoes, Richard. *The Sound of Flutes and Other Indian Legends*. N.Y.: Pantheon, 1976.

Gág, Wanda. *Tales from Grimm*. N.Y.: Coward-McCann, 1936.

Ginsburg, Mirra. *The Kaha Bird: Tales from the Steppes of Central Asia*. N.Y.: Crown, 1971.

Goss, Linda, and Marian E. Barnes. *Talk that Talk: An Anthology of African-American Stories*. N.Y.: Simon and Schuster, 1989.

Hamilton, Virginia. *In The Beginning: Creation Stories from Around the World*. N.Y.: Harcourt Brace Jovanovich, 1988.

————. *The People Could Fly: American Black Folktales*. N.Y.: Knopf, 1985.

Harper, Wilhelmina. *Ghosts & Goblins: Stories for Halloween*. N.Y.: Dutton, 1965.

Haviland, Virginia. *North American Legends*. N.Y.: Collins, 1979.

Jacobs, Joseph. *English Fairy Tales*. N.Y.: Dover, 1967. (Reprint of 1898 edition by Putnam.)

———. *Indian Fairy Tales.* N.Y.: Dover, 1969. (Reprint of 1892 edition by David Nutt.)

Jagendorf, Moritz A. *Upstate Downstate: Folk Stories of the Middle Atlantic States.* N.Y.: Vanguard, 1949.

Jones, Terry. *Fairy Tales.* N.Y.: Schocken, 1981.

Kaye, Danny. *Danny Kaye's Around the World Story Book.* N.Y.: Random House, 1960.

Kennedy, Richard. *Collected Stories.* N.Y.: Harper and Row, 1987.

Leach, Maria. *The Thing at the Foot of the Bed and Other Scary Tales.* N.Y.: World, 1959.

Lester, Julius. *How Many Spots Does a Leopard Have?* N.Y.: Scholastic, 1989.

———. *More Tales of Uncle Remus: Further Adventures of Brer Rabbit, His Friends, Enemies & Others.* N.Y.: Dial, 1988.

———. *The Tales of Uncle Remus.* N.Y.: Dial, 1987.

Livo, Norma, ed. *Joining In: An Anthology of Audience Participation Stories and How to Tell Them.* Cambridge, MA.: Yellow Moon, 1988.

Lurie, Alison. *Clever Gretchen & Other Forgotten Folktales.* N.Y.: Crowell, 1980.

MacDonald, Margaret Read. *Twenty Tellable Tales: Audience Participation Folktales for the Beginning Storyteller.* N.Y.: Wilson, 1986.

———. *When the Lights Go Out: Twenty Scary Tales to Tell.* N.Y.: Wilson, 1988.

Martin, Eva. *Tales of the Far North.* N.Y.: Dial, 1987.

Mayo, Gretchen Will. *Star Tales: North American Indian Stories about the Stars.* N.Y.: Walker, 1987.

Melzack, Ronald. *Raven, Creator of the World.* Boston, MA.: Little, Brown, 1976.

Minard, Rosemary. *Womenfolk & Fairy Tales.* Boston, MA.: Houghton Mifflin, 1975.

Monroe, Jean Guard, and Ray A. Williamson. *They Dance in the Sky.* Boston, MA.: Houghton Mifflin, 1987.

Osborne, Mary Pope. *Favorite Greek Myths.* N.Y.: Scholastic, 1989.

Parks, Van Dyke, adapter and reteller. *Jump Again! More Adventures of Brer Rabbit.* N.Y.: Harcourt Brace Jovanovich, 1987.

———, and Malcolm Jones, adapters and retellers. *Jump! The Adventures of Brer Rabbit.* N.Y.: Harcourt Brace Jovanovich, 1986.

Pellowski, Anne. *The Family Storytelling Handbook: How to Use Stories, Anecdotes, Rhymes, Handkerchiefs, Paper, and Other Objects to Enrich Your Family Traditions*. N.Y.: Macmillan, 1987.

———. *The Story Vine: A Source Book of Unusual and Easy-to-Tell Stories*. N.Y.: Macmillan, 1984.

Phelps, Ethel J. *The Maid of the North: Feminist Folktales from Around the World*. N.Y.: Holt, Rinehart and Winston, 1981.

———. *Tatterhood & Other Tales*. Old Westbury, N.Y.: Feminist Press, 1978.

Russell, William F. *Classic Myths to Read Aloud*. N.Y.: Crown, 1989.

San Souci, Robert D., reteller. *Short & Shivery: Thirty Chilling Tales*. Garden City, N.Y.: Doubleday, 1987.

Schram, Peninnah. *Jewish Stories One Generation Tells Another*. Northvale, N.J.: Aronson, 1987.

Schwartz, Alvin. *More Scary Stories to Tell in the Dark*. N.Y.: Harper and Row, 1984.

———. *Scary Stories to Tell in the Dark*. N.Y.: Harper and Row, 1981.

Schwartz, Howard. *Elijah's Violin & Other Jewish Fairy Tales*. N.Y.: Harper and Row, 1983.

Shannon, George. *Stories to Solve*. N.Y.: Greenwillow, 1985.

Singer, Isaac B. *Zlateh the Goat and other Stories*. N.Y.: Harper and Row, 1966.

Smith, Jimmy Neil, ed. *Homespun: Tales from America's Favorite Storytellers*. N.Y.: Crown, 1988.

Tashjian, Virginia. *Juba This and Juba That*. Boston, MA.: Little, Brown, 1969.

———. *With a Deep Sea Smile*. Boston, MA.: Little, Brown, 1974.

Uchida, Yoshiko. *The Sea of Gold & Other Tales from Japan*. N.Y.: Scribner, 1965.

Untermeyer, Louis. *The Firebringer and Other Great Stories: 55 Legends That Live Forever*. N.Y.: Evans, 1968.

Wolkstein, Diane. *Lazy Stories*. N.Y.: Seabury, 1976.

Yolen, Jane. *Favorite Folktales from Around the World*. N.Y.: Pantheon, 1986.

———. *Neptune Rising: Songs and Tales of the Undersea Folk*. N.Y.: Philomel, 1982.

PICTURE BOOKS

Aardema, Verna. *Who's in Rabbit's House? A Masai Folktale.* N.Y.: Dial, 1977.

————. *Why Mosquitoes Buzz in People's Ears: A West African Tale Retold.* N.Y.: Dial, 1975.

Aruego, Jose, and Ariane Aruego. *A Crocodile's Tale.* N.Y.: Scribner, 1972.

Bang, Molly. *The Old Woman and the Red Pumpkin.* N.Y.: Macmillan, 1975.

————. *Wiley and the Hairy Man.* N.Y.: Macmillan, 1976.

Bernstein, Margery, and Janet Kobrin. *The First Morning: An African Myth.* N.Y.: Scribner, 1976.

Brown, Marcia. *Once a Mouse.* N.Y.: Scribner, 1961.

————. *Stone Soup: An Old Tale.* N.Y.: Scribner, 1947.

Cooper, Susan. *The Selkie Girl.* N.Y.: Margaret K. McElderry, 1986.

DeFelice, Cynthia C. *The Dancing Skeleton.* N.Y.: Macmillan, 1989.

De Paola, Tomie. *Strega Nona.* Englewood Cliffs, N.J.: Prentice-Hall, 1975.

Gág, Wanda. *Millions of Cats.* N.Y.: Coward, McCann and Geoghegan, 1928.

Hardendorff, Jeanne B. *The Bed Just So.* N.Y.: Scholastic, 1977.

Hirsh, Marilyn. *The Rabbi and the 29 Witches: A Talmudic Legend.* N.Y.: Holiday House, 1976.

Hodges, Margaret. *The Wave.* Boston, MA.: Houghton Mifflin, 1964.

Kennedy, Richard. *The Porcelain Man.* Boston, MA.: Little, Brown, 1976.

Lester, Helen. *The Wizard, the Fairy, and the Magic Chicken.* Boston, MA.: Houghton Mifflin, 1983.

Lobel, Anita. *Potatoes, Potatoes.* N.Y.: Harper and Row, 1967.

Lobel, Arnold. *Ming Lo Moves the Mountain.* N.Y.: Greenwillow, 1982.

————. *Mouse Tales.* N.Y.: Harper and Row, 1972.

Marshall, James. *Red Riding Hood.* N.Y.: Dial, 1987.

Miller, Moira. *The Moon Dragon.* N.Y.: Dial, 1989.

Murphy, Jill. *Peace at Last*. N.Y.: Dial, 1980.

San Souci, Robert D. *The Boy and the Ghost*. N.Y.: Simon and Schuster, 1989.

Say, Allen. *Once Under the Cherry Blossom Tree*. N.Y.: Harper and Row, 1974.

Seeger, Pete. *Abiyoyo*. N.Y.: Macmillan, 1986.

Slobodkina, Esphyr. *Caps for Sale*. N.Y.: Scholastic, 1940.

Steptoe, John. *Mufaro's Beautiful Daughters*. N.Y.: Lothrop, Lee and Shepard, 1987.

Titus, Eve. *The Two Stonecutters*. Garden City, N.Y.: Doubleday, 1967.

Tolstoi, Aleksei. *The Great Big Enormous Turnip*. N.Y.: Watts, 1968.

Tresselt, Alvin. *The Mitten*. N.Y.: Lothrop, Lee and Shepard, 1964.

Wolkstein, Diane. *White Wave: A Chinese Tale*. N.Y.: Crowell, 1979.

Zemach, Margot. *It Could Always Be Worse: A Yiddish Folktale Retold*. N.Y.: Scholastic, 1976.

———. *The Three Wishes: An Old Story*. N.Y.: Farrar, Straus and Giroux, 1986.

SUGGESTED STORIES FOR STUDENTS TO TELL

This bibliography includes a variety of types of stories. Our main criteria for the selection was that the story be a good one for telling. Therefore, most of the stories listed are folk tales. We've also included a few stories, such as "Split Pea Soup" by James Marshall and "The Journey" by Arnold Lobel, because they're simple, wonderful stories with which the kids with whom we've worked have always had a lot of success. Almost all of the stories listed are short (one to ten minutes of telling time). Some of these books are out of print, but may be available at your school or local public library or through interlibrary loan.

We have divided the suggestions into two categories: stories for second to fifth graders and for sixth to twelfth graders. The divisions were made primarily because of the subject matter, difficulty, or length of the stories. Even within the stories selected for the second to fifth graders there is a great range of difficulty. We have starred the shortest and simplest stories. You will be the best judge of which stories your students will be able to tell successfully.

GRADES 2–5

Bailey, Carolyn S., and Lewis, Clara M. *Favorite Stories for the Children's Hour*. N.Y.: Platt and Munk, 1965. ("How the Robin's Breast Became Red," "The Sheep and the Pig,"

"The Stone Cutter," "The Story of Arachne," "The Story of Clytie," *"The Wonderful Porridge Pot.")

Baylor, Byrd. *And It Is Still that Way: Legends Told by Arizona Indian Children.* N.Y.: Scribner, 1976. ("The Beautiful Dream," "Coyote Has to Have His Way," *"Coyote in a Hailstorm," *"Coyote Gets Turkey Up a Tree," *"Do You Want to Turn into a Rabbit?," *"Seven Pima Stars," "Why Coyote Isn't Blue," "Why Dogs Don't Talk Anymore.")

Belting, Natalia M. *The Long-tailed Bear and Other Indian Legends.* N.Y.: Bobbs-Merrill, 1961. ("How Crane Got His Long Legs," "How Frogs Lost Their Tails," "How Terrapin's Shell Was Cracked," "How the Birds Came to Have Their Many Colors," "How the Cardinal Got His Red Feathers," "How the Long-tailed Bear Lost His Tail," "How the Whales Reached the Sea," "Why Mole's Front Paws Are Bent.")

————. *The Moon Is a Crystal Ball.* N.Y.: Bobbs-Merrill, 1952. ("The Dancing Brothers," "How the Sun and the Moon and the Wind Went Out to Dinner.")

Botkin, Ben, and Withers, Carl. *The Illustrated Book of American Folklore.* N.Y.: Grosset and Dunlap, 1958. (*"How Coyote Snared the Wind," *"How the Rabbit Lost His Tail.")

Bruchac, Joseph. *Iroquois Stories.* Trumansburg, N.Y.: Crossing, 1985. ("The Coming of Legends," "The Brave Woman and the Flying Head.")

————. *Turkey Brother.* Trumansburg, N.Y.: Crossing, 1975. ("How Bear Lost His Tail.")

Carey, Bonnie. *Baba Yaga's Geese and Other Russian Stories.* Bloomington, IN: Indiana University Press, 1973. (*"The Peasant and the Bear.")

Caswell, Helen Rayburn. *Shadows from the Singing House: Eskimo Folktales.* Rutland, VT.: Tuttle, 1968. ("The Flood," "How the Fog Came," "How the Sea Ravens Came to Be.")

Chang, Isabelle C. *Tales from Old China.* N.Y.: Random House, 1969. (*"The Fox and the Fish," "The Pot.")

Chorao, Kay. *The Baby's Story Book.* N.Y.: Dutton, 1985. (*"The Boy Who Turned Himself into a Peanut," *"The Hare and the Turtle," *"The Lion and the Mouse," *"The Little Red Hen," "The Princess and the Pea," *"The Wind and the Sun.")

Cole, Joanna. *Best Loved Folktales of the World.* Garden City, N.Y.: Doubleday, 1983. ("The Stonecutter.")

Connolly, James E. *Why the Possum's Tail Is Bare and Other North American Indian Nature Tales.* Owings Mills, MD.: Stemmer House, 1985. ("Rabbit Searches for His Dinner," "Why the Possum's Tail Is Bare.")

Cowley, Joy. *Cheer Up, Dad.* Auckland, New Zealand: Shortland, 1980.

De Paola, Tomie. *Strega Nona.* Englewood Cliffs, N.J.: Prentice-Hall, 1975.

Devlin, Harry. *Harry Devlin's Tales of Thunder and Lightning*. N.Y.: Parent's, 1975. (*"The Fool on the Hill.")

Dobbs, Rose. *More Once-Upon-a-Time Stories*. N.Y.: Random House, 1961. ("The Clever Fox," "The Fishes and the Wolf," "The Miser.")

Durell, Ann. *The Diane Goode Book of American Folk Tales and Songs*. N.Y.: Dutton, 1989. ("Davy Crockett Meets His Match," "The Talking Mule.")

Faulkner, William J. *The Days When the Animals Talked*. Chicago, IL.: Follett, 1977 ("Brer Possum and Brer Snake.")

Ginsburg, Mirra. *The Lazies: Tales of the Peoples of Russia*. N.Y.: Macmillan, 1973. (*"The Bird, the Mouse, and the Sausage," "Two Frogs," "Who Will Row Next?")

———. *The Strongest One of All*. N.Y.: Greenwillow, 1977.

———. *Three Rolls and One Doughnut*. N.Y.: Dial, 1970. (*"The Best Liar," *"The Bubble, the Straw, and the Shoe," *"The Cat and the Tiger," "The Peasant and the Bear," *"Plans," *"The Snake and the Fish," "The Traveler's Tale," *"Two Stubborn Goats," *"Which Eye Is Blind.")

———. *The Twelve Clever Brothers and Other Fools*. N.Y.: Lippincott, 1979. (*"The Clever Fool," "The Crooked Pine," "Eight Donkeys," *"How Grandpa Mowed the Lord's Meadow," *"Tyndal Goes to Market," "The Vain Lord.")

———. *Two Greedy Bears*. N.Y.: Macmillan, 1976.

Hardendorff, Jeanne B. *Just One More*. N.Y.: Lippincott, 1969. (*"The Box with Something Pretty in It," "The Crow and the Peacock.")

———. *Tricky Peik and Other Picture Tales*. N.Y.: Lippincott, 1967. (*"Donkey's Eggs," *"The Oyster and the Heron.")

Haviland, Virginia. *Favorite Fairy Tales Told Around the World*. Boston, MA.: Little, Brown, 1955. ("The Three Billy Goats Gruff.")

———. *North American Legends*. N.Y.: Collins, 1979. ("Twist-Mouth Family.")

Jablow, Alta. *The Man in the Moon: Sky Tales from Many Lands*. N.Y.: Holt, Rinehart and Winston, 1969. (*"Fire and the Moon," "Fox and Raven Steal the Moon," *"Getting the Moon Back into the Sky," "The Greedy Man in the Moon," "Why the Sun and the Moon Live in the Sky," *"Why the Sun Shines in the Daytime and the Moon Shines at Night.")

Johnson, Edna. *Anthology of Children's Literature*. Boston, MA.: Houghton Mifflin, 1959. ("The Real Princess.")

Jones, Terry. *Fairy Tales*. N.Y.: Schocken, 1981. ("Brave Molly.")

Jonsen, George. *Favorite Tales of Monsters and Trolls*. N.Y.: Random House, 1977. ("The Stone Cheese.")

Kaula, Edna Mason. *African Village Folktales*. Cleveland, OH.: World, 1968. ("How Frog Lost His Tail," "Lion, Chameleon, and Chicken," "The Mighty Warrior in Hare's House," "Lion and Honey Badger," "The Pattern on Tortoise's Back.")

Kaye, Danny. *Danny Kaye's Around the World Story Book*. N.Y.: Random House, 1960. ("The Big Oven," "The Cat Who Used His Head," "The First Noses," "The Vegetable Tree," "Why Wisdom Is Found Everywhere.")

Kent, Jack. *More Fables of Aesop*. N.Y.: Parent's, 1974. (*"The Crow and the Pitcher," *"The Hare and the Tortoise," *"The Lion and the Mouse.")

Krause, Ruth. *The Carrot Seed*. N.Y.: Harper and Row, 1945.

Leach, Maria. *The Lion Sneezed: Folktales and Myths of the Cat*. N.Y.: Crowell, 1977. (*"Why Cat Eats First and Washes Afterward," *"Why Goat Cannot Climb a Tree.")

————. *Noodles, Nitwits and Numskulls*. N.Y.: World, 1961. (*"The Horse with His Head Where His Tail Ought to Be," *"Rescuing the Moon," *"Telling the Horses Apart," *"Three Dreams.")

————. *The Rainbow Book of American Folk Tales and Legends*. N.Y.: World, 1958. (*"Fire.")

————. *The Thing at the Foot of the Bed and Other Scary Tales*. N.Y.: World, 1959. (*"Dark, Dark, Dark," *"Don't Ever Kick a Ghost," "The Golden Arm," *"I'm in the Room!" "The Legs," *"The Lucky Man," "Wait Till Martin Comes.")

————. *Whistle in the Graveyard: Folktales to Chill Your Bones*. N.Y.: Viking, 1974. ("I'm Coming Up the Stairs," "Nobody Here But You and Me.")

Lester, Julius. *The Knee-high Man and Other Tales*. N.Y.: Dial, 1972. ("The Farmer and the Snake," "What Is Trouble?" "Why Dogs Hate Cats," "Why the Waves Have Whitecaps.")

Lobel, Arnold. *Fables*. N.Y.: Harper and Row, 1980. ("The Bad Kangaroo," "King Lion and the Beetle.")

————. *Mouse Tales*. N.Y.: Harper and Row, 1972. (*"Clouds," *"The Journey," *"The Old Mouse," *"Very Tall Mouse and Very Short Mouse," *"The Wishing Well.")

Manning-Sanders, Ruth. *Tortoise Tales*. Nashville, TN.: Nelson, 1972. ("Little Cat and Little Hen," "Tortoise and Ogre.")

Marshall, James. *George and Martha*. Boston, MA.: Houghton Mifflin, 1974. (*"Split Pea Soup.")

————. *Tons of Fun*. Boston, MA.: Houghton Mifflin, 1980. (*"The Sweet Tooth.")

Mayo, Gretchen Will. *Star Tales: North American Indian Stories about the Stars*. N.Y.: Walker, 1987. ("Coyote Makes the Constellations.")

McDermott, Gerald. *The Stonecutter: A Japanese Folk Tale*. N.Y.: Viking, 1975.

Melser, June, and Joy Cowley. *One Cold Wet Night*. Auckland, New Zealand: Shortland, 1980.

Montgomerie, Norah. *Twenty-five Fables*. N.Y.: Abelard-Schuman, 1961. ("The Date Gatherers," *"The Little Grey Goose," *"The Monkey and the Shark," "The Robin and the Wren," *"The Tortoise and the Two Swans.")

Morimoto, Junko. *Mouse's Marriage*. N.Y.: Viking Kestrel, 1986.

Murphy, Jill. *Peace at Last*. N.Y.: Dial, 1980.

Oxenbury, Helen. *The Helen Oxenbury Nursery Story Book*. N.Y.: Knopf, 1985. ("The Elves and the Shoemaker," "The Gingerbread Boy," "Goldilocks and the Three Bears," "The Little Red Hen," "Little Red Riding Hood.")

Rice, Eve. *Once in a Wood: Ten Tales from Aesop*. N.Y.: Greenwillow, 1979. (*"The Crow and the Water Jug," *"The Fox and the Crow," "The Fox and the Goat," "The Frog and the Ox," *"The Fox and the Stork," *"The Hare Who Had Many Friends," "The Lion and the Fox," *"The Lion and the Mouse.")

Rockwell, Anne. *The Old Woman and Her Pig and Ten Other Stories*. N.Y.: Crowell, 1979. ("The Travels of a Fox.")

————. *The Three Bears and 15 Other Stories*. N.Y.: Crowell, 1975. (*"The Dog and the Bone," *"The Lion and the Mouse," "The Little Pot," "Teeny-Tiny," "The Three Billy Goats Gruff," "The Three Bears," "The Gingerbread Man," "The Water Nixie," "The Shoemaker and the Elves," "The Three Little Pigs," "Lazy Jack," "Little Red Riding Hood.")

Schwartz, Alvin. *In a Dark, Dark Room and Other Scary Stories*. N.Y.: Harper and Row, 1984. ("The Night It Rained," *"The Pirate.")

————. *More Scary Stories to Tell in the Dark*. N.Y.: Harper and Row, 1984. (*"Cemetery Soup.")

————. *Scary Stories to Tell in the Dark*. N.Y.: Harper and Row, 1981. (*"The Viper.")

Slobodkina, Esphyr. *Caps for Sale*. N.Y.: Scholastic, 1940.

Stevens, Bryna. *Borrowed Feathers and Other Fables*. N.Y.: Random House, 1977. (*"The Fox and the Crow," *"The Fox and the Goat," *"The Great and Little Fishes," *"The Milkmaid," *"The North Wind and the Sun," *"The Stag and His Reflection.")

Tall Book of Nursery Tales, The. N.Y.: Harper and Row, 1944. ("The City Mouse and the Country Mouse," *"The Foolish Milkmaid," "The Fox and the Crow," "The Straw, the Coal, and the Bean," *"The Goose that Laid the Golden Eggs," "The Wolf and the Kids," "Wolf! Wolf!")

Thorne, Ian. *Monster Tales of Native Americans.* Mankato, MN.: Crestwood House, 1978. ("The River Monster," "Thunderer and the Fever-Monster.")

Todd, Loreto. *Tortoise the Trickster and Other Folk Tales from Cameroon.* N.Y.: Schocken, 1979. (*"Stubbornness Causes Trouble," "Wisdom Belongs to Everyone.")

Wilson, Barbara Ker. *Animal Folk Tales.* N.Y.: Grosset and Dunlap, 1971. ("The Cat and Her Pupil," "The Swimming Race.")

Wolkstein, Diane. *The Magic Orange Tree and Other Haitian Folktales.* N.Y.: Knopf, 1978. ("Bye-Bye.")

Wyndham, Lee. *Tales the People Tell in Russia.* N.Y.: Messner, 1970. ("The Woodcutter and the Water Demon.")

Yeatman, Linda. *A Treasury of Animal Stories.* N.Y.: Simon and Schuster, 1982. ("The Dragon and the Monkey," "Elephant and Rabbit," *"The Lion and the Mouse," "A Lion in the Meadow," "The Little House," "The Little Red Hen and the Fox," "The Little Jackal and the Crocodile.")

Yolen, Jane. *Favorite Folktales from Around the World.* N.Y.: Pantheon, 1986. ("The Monkey and the Crocodile.")

Zaum, Marjorie. *Catlore: Tales from Around the World.* N.Y.: Atheneum, 1985. ("Why the Cat Washes His Paws After Eating.")

Zemach, Margot. *The Three Wishes: An Old Story.* N.Y.: Farrar, Straus and Giroux, 1986.

Ziskind, Sylvia. *Telling Stories to Children.* N.Y.: Wilson, 1976. (*"The Little Cream Cheese.")

GRADES 6–12

Arnott, Kathleen. *African Myths and Legends.* N.Y.: Walck, 1963. ("The Monkey's Heart.")

Babbitt, Natalie. *The Devil's Storybook.* N.Y.: Farrar, Straus and Giroux, 1974. ("Ashes," "Wishes.")

Bailey, Carolyn S., and Clara M. Lewis. *Favorite Stories for the Children's Hour.* N.Y.: Platt and Munk, 1965. ("The Farmer and the Troll.")

Belting, Natalia. *The Moon Is a Crystal Ball.* N.Y.: Bobbs-Merrill, 1952. ("White Hawk and the Star Maidens.")

Bernstein, Margery, and Janet Korbin. *Earth Namer.* N.Y.: Scribner, 1974.

Borski, Lucia Merecka. *Good Sense and Good Fortune/and Other Polish Folk Tales.* N.Y.: David McKay, 1970. ("The Wise Witness.")

Bruchac, Joseph. *Turkey Brother.* Trumansburg, N.Y.: Crossing, 1975. ("How Bear Lost His Tail.")

Caswell, Helen Rayburn. *Shadows from the Singing House: Eskimo Folktales.* Rutland, VT.: Tuttle, 1968. ("The Man and the Star.")

Chang, Isabelle C. *Tales from Old China.* N.Y.: Random House, 1969. ("The Shady Tree," "Unanswerable Questions.")

Cole, Joanna. *Best Loved Folktales of the World.* Garden City, N.Y.: Doubleday, 1983. ("The Clever Thief," "The Donkey Driver and the Thief," "Hats to Disappear With," "Molly Whuppie.")

Connolly, James E. *Why the Possum's Tail Is Bare and Other North American Indian Nature Tales.* Owings Mills, MD.: Stemmer House, 1985. ("The Hermit Thrush," "How the Turtle Beat the Rabbit.")

Courlander, Harold. *The King's Drum and Other African Stories.* N.Y.: Harcourt Brace Jovanovich, 1962. ("The Chief of the Gurensi," "The King's Drum," "The Feast," "The Wedding of the Hawk.")

————. *The Tiger's Whisker and Other Tales and Legends from Asia and the Pacific.* N.Y.: Harcourt Brace Jovanovich, 1959. ("The Tiger's Whisker.")

Ginsburg, Mirra. *The Lazies: Tales of the Peoples of Russia.* N.Y.: Macmillan, 1973. ("The Clever Thief," "Two Frogs.")

Hardendorff, Jeanne B. *Just One More.* N.Y.: Lippincott, 1969. ("The Most Frugal of Men," "The Princess Who Learned to Work," "The Wolf and the Blacksmith.")

————. *Tricky Peik and Other Picture Tales.* N.Y.: Lippincott, 1967. ("Donkey's Eggs.")

————. *Witches, Wit and a Werewolf.* N.Y.: Lippincott, 1971. ("The Little Toe Bone," "Rap! Rap! Rap!," "Vengeance Will Come.")

Hogrogian, Nonny. *One Fine Day.* N.Y.: Macmillan, 1971.

Jablow, Alta. *The Man in the Moon: Sky Tales from Many Lands.* N.Y.: Holt, Rinehart and Winston, 1969. ("The Owl in the Moon.")

Jacobs, Joseph. *English Fairy Tales.* N.Y.: Dover, 1967. ("Mr. Fox.")

Jones, Terry. *Fairy Tales.* N.Y.: Schocken, 1981. ("The Corn Dolly," "The Glass Cupboard," "The Sea Tiger," "The Wonderful Cake-Horse.")

Kaye, Danny. *Danny Kaye's Around the World Story Book*. N.Y.: Random House, 1960. ("The Alligator's Courtship," "Anansi and the Baboon," "The Best Meal and the Worst," "Bouqui and the Enormous Yams," "The Camel and the Cat," "The Conceited Spider," "The Coyote and the Dogs," "The Judgement of Karakoush," "The Maiden of the Sea," "The Talented Companions," "The Talking Eggs.")

Leach, Maria. *The Thing at the Foot of the Bed and Other Scary Tales*. N.Y.: World, 1959. ("Aunt Tilly," "The Cradle that Rocked by Itself," "The Gangster in the Back Seat," "The Ghostly Hitchhiker," "The Head," "Milk Bottles," "Talk.")

————. *Whistle in the Graveyard: Folktales to Chill Your Bones*. N.Y.: Viking, 1974. ("Anne Boleyn," "Bill Is with Me Now," "The Black Cat's Eyes," "Blackbeard's Treasure," "Can't Rest," "Crossing the Bridge," "The Ghost on Brass's Hill," "The Ghostly Spools," "Grandpa Joe's Brother," "How to Become a Witch," "One Handful," "The Sea Captain at the Door," "The Tired Ghost," "Tony and His Harp.")

Lurie, Alison. *Clever Gretchen and Other Forgotten Folktales*. N.Y.: Crowell, 1980. ("The Hand of Glory," "Manka and the Judge.")

Matson, Emerson N. *Longhouse Legends*. Camden, N.J.: Thomas Nelson, 1968. ("The Raven and the Crow," "Sam Dan and the Government Doctor.")

McCarty, Toni. *The Skull in the Snow and Other Folktales*. N.Y.: Delacorte, 1981. ("Fatima and the Tiger.")

Musick, Ruth Ann. *The Telltale Lilac Bush and Other West Virginia Ghost Tales*. Lexington, KY.: University of Kentucky Press, 1965. ("The Boy and the Trumpet," "Footsteps on the Walk," "Help," "The Little Rag Doll," "A Loyal Dog," "The Phantom Soldier," "Rapping on the Door," "Rose Run," "Strange Noises," "The Upstairs Bedroom.")

Phelps, Ethel Johnston. *Tatterhood and Other Tales*. Old Westbury, N.Y.: Feminist Press, 1978. ("The Giant Caterpillar," "The Hunted Hare.")

Protter, Eric. *A Children's Treasury of Folk and Fairy Tales*. N.Y.: Beaufort, 1982. ("The Czar's General and the Clever Peasant," "The Pastor and the Sexton," "The Wishing Ring.")

Riordan, James. *The Woman in the Moon and Other Tales of Forgotten Heroines*. N.Y.: Dial, 1985. ("The Nagging Husband.")

Roessel, Robert A., Jr. *Coyote Stories of the Navajo People*. Phoenix, AZ.: Navajo Curriculum Center Press, 1974. ("Coyote and the Doe," "Coyote and the Porcupine.")

Schwartz, Alvin. *More Scary Stories to Tell in the Dark*. N.Y.: Harper and Row, 1984. ("The Bad News," "The Bed by the Window," "The Bride," "The Brown Suit," "The Cat in a Shopping Bag," "The Cat's Paw," "Clinkity-Clink," "The Drum," "The Little Black Dog," "Rings on Her Fingers," "Somebody Fell from Aloft," "Something Was Wrong," "One Sunday Morning," "The Window.")

————. *Scary Stories to Tell in the Dark*. N.Y.: Harper and Row, 1981. ("Alligators," "Cold as Clay," "The Guests," "The Haunted House," "High Beams," "Room for One More," "What Do You Come For?," "The White Satin Evening Gown.")

Sharma, Partap. *The Surangini Tales*. N.Y.: Harcourt Brace Jovanovich, 1973. ("The Wisdom of the Rubber Ball.")

Thorne, Ian. *Monster Tales of Native Americans*. Mankato, MN.: Crestwood House, 1978. ("The Frogs of Forbidden Mountain," "The Little People," "The Spirit Lake Demons.")

Thurber, James. *The Thurber Carnival*. N.Y.: Delta, 1931. ("The Little Girl and the Wolf," "The Moth and the Star.")

Walker, Barbara. *Watermelons, Walnuts and the Wisdom of Allah and Other Tales of the Hoca*. N.Y.: Parent's, 1967. ("Eat, My Fine Coat," "The Hoca Solves a Problem," How Long Will It Take?," "The Sound Is Yours.")

Wilson, Barbara Ker. *Animal Folk Tales*. N.Y.: Grosset and Dunlap, 1971. ("The Fox Outwits the Lion," "The Greedy Dog.")

Wolkstein, Diane. *White Wave*. N.Y.: Crowell, 1979.

Yeatman, Linda. *A Treasury of Animal Stories*. N.Y.: Simon and Schuster, 1982. ("Pegasus, the Winged Horse.")

Yolen, Jane. *Favorite Folktales from Around the World*. N.Y.: Pantheon, 1986. ("The Flying Head," "The Happy Man's Shirt," "How Mosquitoes Came to Be," "The Old Lady in the Cave," "The Old Man and His Grandson," "The Two Pickpockets.")

Appendix B

Twenty-five Stories for Children to Tell

ABOUT THE STORIES

We've included a section of stories to help get you started. Many of these are simple and short, since we have found that it's difficult to find stories that are easy enough for younger children to tell. The stories are arranged in order of difficulty, beginning with the simplest.

HOW THE RABBIT LOST HIS TAIL

Once the rabbit met the fox carrying a long string of fish.

"Where did you get all those nice fish, Mr. Fox?" asked the rabbit.

The fox offered to teach the rabbit how to catch fish too, and took him down to a hole in the ice. "You sit here all night with your tail hanging down in the water," the fox said, "and in the morning you'll have a nice string of fish on your tail."

But in the morning the rabbit's tail was frozen tight in the ice. He pulled and pulled, but he couldn't get loose. The owl came and pulled him first by one ear and then by the other. The rabbit's ears stretched out long, but he still stuck. Finally his friends pulled him loose, but his tail pulled off and stuck in the ice. That's why the rabbit has such long ears and such a short tail.

Retold by Ben Botkin and Carl Withers in *The Illustrated Book of American Folklore* (N.Y.: Grosset and Dunlap, 1958).

THE SUN AND THE WIND
A FABLE OF AESOP

One day the Sun and the Wind got into a big quarrel over which one was the strongest.

"I am the most powerful," said the Sun.

"No, I am the most powerful!" argued the Wind.

While they were arguing, they saw a man wearing a cape walking down the road.

"Here is a chance to test our strength," said the Wind. "Let us see which of us is strong enough to make that man take off his cape."

"Agreed," said the Sun.

So the Sun went behind a cloud and the Wind took his turn first. He huffed and he puffed, but the harder he blew, the tighter the man held his cape around him. The Wind could not get the cape off no matter how hard he tried, and at last he had to give up.

Then it was the Sun's turn. He came out from behind the cloud and began to shine his warmest rays down on the man. As it grew hotter and hotter the man unfastened his cape and let it hang loosely around his shoulders. Finally, he took it off completely.

The Sun had done with kindness what the Wind could not do with force.

Retold by Martha Hamilton and Mitch Weiss—Beauty & the Beast Storytellers.
© 1990 Martha Hamilton and Mitch Weiss—Beauty & the Beast Storytellers. *Children Tell Stories: A Teaching Guide*. Richard C. Owen Publishers, Inc., Katonah, New York. All rights reserved.

THE FROG AND THE OX
A FABLE OF AESOP

A small Frog came hopping home as fast as he could go. When he saw a large old Frog sitting beside the pond, he called out, "I have just seen such a terrible monster; it was as big as a mountain, with a long tail and horns on its head. Look, he's over in the meadow."

The old Frog looked. "Oh, that's nothing," he replied. "Why that's only Farmer White's Ox. He isn't so very big. Why I could easily make myself as big as he. Just you watch."

So the old Frog took a deep, deep breath and puffed out his chest. Then he asked, "Was the Ox as big as this?"

"Oh, much bigger than that," said the young Frog.

Again the old one took a deep, deep breath and swelled himself out even more.

"Was the Ox bigger than this?"

"Oh, much, much bigger," said the little Frog.

So the old Frog took a very, very, very deep breath, and he swelled and swelled even more than before. And then he said, "I'm sure the Ox is not as big as me!"

But just then—POP!—he burst!

The small Frog thought, "What a fool! He tried to be bigger than he was, and now there's *nothing* left of him."

Retold by Martha Hamilton and Mitch Weiss—Beauty & the Beast Storytellers.
© 1990 Martha Hamilton and Mitch Weiss—Beauty & the Beast Storytellers. *Children Tell Stories: A Teaching Guide*. Richard C. Owen Publishers, Inc., Katonah, New York. All rights reserved.

THE DOG AND HIS SHADOW
A FABLE OF AESOP

It happened that one day a dog was taking a walk through town and he passed the butcher shop. He could not help but notice all the delicious looking soup bones that the butcher had put in the window to sell to his customers. Quick as a flash the dog stole one of the bones and ran off, with the butcher close at his heels.

The dog soon left the butcher far behind, but he did not stop running until he was out of town. He headed for his home, where he knew he could eat the bone without anyone bothering him.

Now on his way home he had to cross a bridge over a clear stream. As he crossed the bridge he stopped and looked down at the water below. There, in the water, he saw his own reflection, but he thought it was another dog with a soup bone. And the other dog's bone looked bigger and better than the one he had stolen from the butcher. So the greedy dog made up his mind to have the other bone as well.

He snarled at the dog in the water and, sure enough, the other dog snarled right back at him. Then he decided to make a grab for the other dog's bone. But as he opened his mouth his bone fell right into the stream and disappeared from sight. And that greedy dog felt very foolish and very hungry for the rest of the day.

THE BOY WHO TURNED HIMSELF
INTO A PEANUT

One day a little boy decided to fool his father. "I will hide myself so well that you will not be able to find me," he said.

"Hide wherever you like," said the father. "I will just go home now and take a rest."

So the boy looked for a hiding place.

He saw a peanut that had three kernels, so he turned himself into one of the kernels and hid in the peanut.

Just then a rooster came along and swallowed the peanut.

Then a wild bush cat leaped on the rooster and swallowed him.

Then a dog saw the bush cat and, after a long chase, gobbled him down.

The dog was sleeping when a python slithered by and made a meal of him.

The python went down to the river and was caught in a fish trap.

Meanwhile, the father had finished resting and was looking everywhere for his son. Not seeing him, he walked to the river to inspect his fish trap.

There he found a large python, which he opened and found a dog. He opened the dog and found a bush cat. He opened the bush cat and found a rooster. He opened the rooster and found a peanut.

Of course, when he opened the peanut, out jumped his son! The boy was so surprised to be found that he never tried to fool his father again.

Retold by Kay Chorao in *The Baby's Story Book* (N.Y.: Dutton, 1985).

THE LITTLE PORRIDGE POT
A GERMAN FOLK TALE FROM
THE BROTHERS GRIMM

There was once a young girl who lived with her mother. They were quite poor and often did not have enough to eat. One day they found their cupboards completely empty.

The little girl went off into the forest in search of wild fruit and berries. She was so busy filling her basket that she did not notice an old woman watching her. At last the old woman stepped out and said: "I can see that you are very hungry. There is no need to look so troubled. Take this pot home and you shall always have enough food. It is magic! When you say to it 'Cook, little pot, cook,' it will fill up with good sweet porridge. And when you have had enough, just say, 'Stop, little pot, stop.'"

The girl could not believe her good fortune. She thanked the woman for her kindness and hurried home to show her mother the pot. After this, life was much easier for the woman and her daughter. Whenever their food ran low they could eat sweet porridge.

One day the girl went off to play with some of her friends. While she was gone her mother grew very hungry and decided to have a small meal of porridge. She said to the pot, "Cook, little pot, cook," and sure enough it wasn't long before the pot was full of porridge. She filled her bowl and sat down to eat. As she was eating, she suddenly realized that she hadn't told the pot to stop. She jumped up and ran to the pot, which was just beginning to overflow; but in her excitement the mother could not remember the magic words to stop the pot.

All she could do was helplessly watch the porridge pour onto the floor. On and on the pot cooked, until the house was full of porridge and it flowed out the door and windows. It wasn't long before all the houses in her neighborhood were filled to the top with porridge. If the woman didn't remember the magic words soon the whole village would be covered with porridge.

Still the pot cooked and still the porridge kept coming. At last it reached the house where the little girl was playing. When she saw the streets filled with porridge she ran home as quickly as she could, which was very difficult with porridge up to her knees.

When she arrived home she called out, "Stop, little pot, stop!" And sure enough, the pot stopped bubbling.

For the next month the people in that town ate nothing but porridge—porridge pancakes, porridge sandwiches, and porridge pies. You can be sure the mother learned the magic words and never forgot them.

THE TORTOISE WHO TALKED
TOO MUCH
AN INDIAN FABLE

Long, long ago a tortoise lived in a pond with two swans, who were her very good friends. She enjoyed the company of the swans, because she could talk with them to her heart's content, for the tortoise loved to talk. She always had something to say, and she liked to hear herself say it.

After many years of living happily in the pond there came a dry season. There was no rain for weeks and weeks, and at last the pond dried up completely. The two swans realized they would have to leave their home and fly to another pond that held water. So they went to say good-bye to their friend, the tortoise.

But she begged them, "Don't leave me behind! I too have nothing to eat and no water to live on. I will surely die if I am left here."

"But you can't fly!" said the swans. "How can we take you with us?"

"Take me with you! Please take me with you!" pleaded the tortoise.

The swans felt so sorry for their friend that at last they came up with a plan. They said to the tortoise, "We have thought of a way to take you with us. We will each take hold of one end of a long stick. You must hold onto it with your teeth and never let go. You must not talk as long as we are carrying you! If you open your mouth you'll surely fall to the ground."

The tortoise promised not to say a word. And the swans flew slowly into the air carrying the tortoise on the stick between them.

As they rose above the treetops tortoise wanted to say, "Goodness, look how high we are!" But she remembered, and kept still.

Soon they passed over a small town and a few people looked up and saw them.

"Look at the swans carrying a tortoise!" they shouted, and everyone ran to look.

The tortoise wanted to say to the swans, "Why don't they mind their own business?" But she held her tongue.

Then the people began to shout, "Look at that! How strange! Look, everybody!"

The tortoise could stand it no longer. She opened her mouth to call out, "Hush, you foolish people!" But as she did, she fell to the ground. She landed on her back and her shell cracked in a thousand pieces.

Tortoise's shell has remained that way to this day. Her cracked shell reminds us of what can happen if we talk too much.

THE LITTLE HOUSE
A RUSSIAN FOLK TALE

Once upon a time a jar rolled off a farmer's cart and was left lying in the middle of a field. A little mouse came running along and saw the jar lying there, and thought what a nice house it would make and began to wonder who lived there.

The little mouse said, "Little house, little house, who lives in this little house?"

Nobody answered. Then the little mouse looked in, and found no one there!

"Well, then," he said, "I shall live here myself." So he settled himself in the jar.

Then a frog came hopping along and said, "Little house, little house, who lives in this little house?"

"I, Mr. Mouse, I live in this little house, and what sort of animal are you?"

"I am Mr. Frog."

"Come inside then, and let's live together."

"Very well, let's."

So the frog crept into the jar, and they began to live together.

Then a hare came running over the field.

"Little house, little house," says he, "who lives in this little house?"

"Mr. Frog and Mr. Mouse, and who are you?"

"I am Mr. Hare who runs over the hills. May I come in too?"

"Yes, you may. Come and live here; there's plenty of room."

Then a fox came running past and said, "Little house, little house, who lives in this little house?"

"Mr. Hare, Mr. Frog, and Mr. Mouse. And what is your name?"

"They call me Mr. Fox."

"Very well then, come and live with us."

"Right you are!"

So the fox got into the jar too, and all four began to live together. And they went on living there, until suddenly a bear came along out of the forest and said, "Little house, little house, who lives in this little house?"

"Mr. Fox, Mr. Hare, Mr. Frog, and Mr. Mouse, and who are you?"

"I am Mr. Bear-Squash-You-All-Flat." And the bear sat down on the jar and squashed it flat.

And that was the end of the little house.

Adapted from Valery Carrick, Nevill Forbes trans. *Picture Tales from the Russian* (N.Y.: Lippin-cott, 1913).
© 1990 Martha Hamilton and Mitch Weiss—Beauty & the Beast Storytellers. *Children Tell Stories: A Teaching Guide.* Richard C. Owen Publishers, Inc., Katonah, New York. All rights reserved.

COYOTE AND THE MONEY TREE

Coyote had some money, just a few dollars. He was walking down a road trying to figure out how to change those dollars into something more valuable.

Coming toward him were some American prospectors with their horses and mules and blankets and guns and bags of food.

Coyote had a brilliant thought. He put his money up in the branches of a tree that was growing beside the road. Then he just sat there watching the tree.

When the American prospectors rode up they asked him, "What are you doing?"

"I am watching this tree. It is very valuable," Coyote said.

"Why is it valuable? What is in that tree?" the prospectors asked.

"Money grows on that tree," Coyote said. "When I shake it money falls out."

The prospectors laughed at him so Coyote shook the tree a little and one of his dollars fell out.

Now the men were very interested. "Sell us that tree," they said.

"No," Coyote said, pretending to be angry. "This is the only tree in the world that grows money."

The prospectors said, "We will give you everything we have—our horses and mules and everything else. We will just climb down and you will own everything."

Coyote still pretended not to want to, and the prospectors tried to persuade him.

But after a while Coyote let them persuade him. "All right," he said. "I will sell you the tree. There is only one thing."

"Anything at all," they said.

"See those blue mountains over there? Well, you will have to wait until I get there. If you shake the tree before that, nothing will come out and you will spoil it forever."

The prospectors agreed.

So Coyote jumped on one of the horses and rode away with everything they had.

When Coyote had reached the blue mountains the men shook the tree. Only one dollar fell out though they shook and shook and shook. That was the last dollar Coyote had put there.

Over by the blue mountains Coyote was laughing.

HOW THE MILKY WAY BEGAN

If you look almost directly above you on a starry night you will see a white band of light that trails clear across the sky. That is the Milky Way. It looks like a million tiny grains of dust. But the Milky Way is really a great band of individual stars. Some are very large. Some are a little smaller. And here is a story—told sometimes in Persia, sometimes in Africa—of the way the Milky Way began.

Once there lived a man who was both greedy and sly. If he needed a thing, like a horse or a sheep, he would not work to get it. He would steal it from his neighbors instead.

Now one day this man needed a load of straw. He could have harvested the fields as his neighbors did, but instead he took his horse and cart, crept into his neighbor's field in the dead of night and stole that load of straw.

Since he was unused to work he took some time to load the straw in his wagon. By the time he had finished, the great golden sun was beginning its climb across the sky and all the people were waking from their dark night of sleep. Where could he hide his great load of straw so that it would not be seen?

He looked this way and he looked that way, but could find no place to hide his wagon. Then he looked up, and there was the wide, blue sky above him, and no one was in it at all. The very place to hide! He lashed his horse, and away he flew. Up, up he went, until he was sailing across the very middle of the sky! He flew faster and faster so that no one might see where he was hiding his precious load.

The day passed, and when the sun had made his trip across the blue sky and settled behind the hills of the earth—lo and behold!—the man had disappeared and his stolen straw with him. Now no one would find him.

But wait a moment! The man, as you know, had hurried across the sky; and as he hurried, some pieces of the straw had dropped out of his cart. There they were across the middle of the sky, showing the path he had taken.

Look up into the sky any clear night, and you will see a golden path of shining straw. You may not be able to find the man—the man who was greedy and sly—but you'll know which way he went.

Retold by Eva Knox Evans. *Out of the Sky* (Publication Committee, West Georgia College, 1944).

THE RAT PRINCESS
A JAPANESE FOLK TALE

Once upon a time there was a Rat Princess who lived with her father, the Rat King, and her mother, the Rat Queen, in a rice field in faraway Japan. The Rat Princess was very beautiful, and her parents loved her so much that they thought no one was good enough to play with her. When she grew up, they wouldn't let any of the Rat Princes come to visit her. They wanted her to have the best and the mightiest husband in the world, so the Rat King set out to find him.

First he went to the Sun and said, "I have come to offer you the hand of my daughter, the Princess, in marriage because only you can make the rice grow and ripen. You are the most powerful being in the world."

But the Sun replied, "Thank you for thinking of me, but I am not the most powerful. When the Cloud passes over me, I cannot shine."

So the Rat King went and asked the Cloud to marry his daughter. But the Cloud replied, "I am not the most powerful being. The Wind is stronger than I am. When he blows, I have to go wherever he sends me.

Next the Rat King traveled until he found the Wind and asked him to marry his daughter.

"Oh, you should ask the Wall, for he is far more powerful than I. No matter how hard I blow, I can never move the Wall."

And so the Rat King came down from the sky and traveled across the earth until he came to the Wall. It was quite near his own rice field. He asked the Wall to marry his daughter.

"I am not the strongest," grumbled the Wall. "The big gray Rat who lives in the cellar is stronger than I. He gnaws and gnaws at me with his sharp teeth, and at last I crumble. You must go to the Rat and ask him to marry your daughter."

The Rat King thought to himself, "How is it that I didn't realize sooner that we rats are the most powerful creatures on this earth!"

And so, after going all over the world to find the best and mightiest husband, the Rat King married his daughter to a rat after all. As for the Princess, she was quite pleased, since she had wanted to marry a rat all along.

Retold by Martha Hamilton and Mitch Weiss—Beauty & the Beast Storytellers.
© 1990 Martha Hamilton and Mitch Weiss—Beauty & the Beast Storytellers. *Children Tell Stories: A Teaching Guide*. Richard C. Owen Publishers, Inc., Katonah, New York. All rights reserved.

THE MAN, THE BOY, AND THE DONKEY
A FABLE OF AESOP

A man and his son were once going to market with their donkey. As they were walking along by its side a gentleman passed them and said, "You fools, what is a donkey for but to ride upon?"

So the man put the boy on the donkey and they went on their way. But soon they passed a group of men, one of whom said, "See that lazy youngster, he lets his father walk while he rides."

So the man ordered his boy to get off, and got on himself. But they hadn't gone far when they passed two women, one of whom said to the other, "How can that father ride on the donkey while his poor son can hardly keep up with them?"

Well, the man didn't know what to do, but at last he took his son up in front of him on the donkey. They had now almost reached the town when a fellow stopped the man and asked, "Sir, is that your donkey?"

"It certainly is," replied the man.

"I would never have thought so from the way you are loading the poor beast down. Why, you two fellows would be able to carry him more easily than he can carry you! You should be ashamed of yourselves!"

The man and the boy got off the donkey. Then they cut down a pole, tied the donkey's feet to it, and raised the pole and the donkey to their shoulders. They started walking across a bridge which led into the town, and a huge crowd of people gathered to laugh at them. The donkey, who did not like all the noise or his situation, kicked the rope away and tumbled off the pole and into the river and drowned.

The man, who was both angry and ashamed, turned and headed home. He realized that by trying to please everybody he had pleased nobody, and lost his donkey in the bargain.

Adapted from Joseph Jacobs. *The Fables of Aesop.* (London: Macmillan, 1912).
© 1990 Martha Hamilton and Mitch Weiss—Beauty & the Beast Storytellers. *Children Tell Stories: A Teaching Guide.* Richard C. Owen Publishers, Inc., Katonah, New York. All rights reserved.

THE THREE GOATS
A NORWEGIAN FOLK TALE

There once was a boy who had three goats. All day they leaped and pranced and skipped and climbed up on the rocky hill, but at night the boy drove them home. One night, when he went to meet them, the frisky things leaped into a turnip field and he could not get them out. Then the boy sat down on the hillside and cried.

As he sat there a rabbit came along. "Why are you crying?" asked the rabbit.

"I'm crying because I can't get the goats out of the field," answered the boy.

"*I'll* do it," said the rabbit. So he tried, but the goats would not come. Then the rabbit too sat down and cried.

Along came a fox. "Why are you crying?" asked the fox.

"I am crying because the boy cries," said the rabbit; "and the boy is crying because he cannot get the goats out of the turnip field."

"*I'll* do it," said the fox.

So the fox tried, but the goats would not come. Then the fox also sat down and cried.

Soon after, a wolf came along. "Why are you crying?" asked the wolf.

"I am crying because the rabbit cries," said the fox; "and the rabbit cries because the boy cries; and the boy cries because he can't get the goats out of the turnip field."

"*I'll* do it," said the wolf.

He tried. But the goats would not leave the field. So he sat down beside the others and began to cry too.

After a little, a bee flew over the hill and saw them all sitting there crying. "Why are you crying?" said the bee to the wolf.

"I am crying because the fox cries; and the fox cries because the rabbit cries; and the rabbit cries because the boy cries; and the boy cries because he can't get the goats out of the turnip field."

"*I'll* do it," said the bee.

Then the big animals and the boy all stopped crying a moment to laugh at the tiny bee. How could *he* possibly do it, when they couldn't! But the tiny bee flew away into the turnip field and stung one of the goats.

And out ran the goats, every one!

THE RICH MAN'S GUEST
A TURKISH FOLK TALE

Many years ago there lived a very wise king in a country far from here. One day while he was out riding he passed a beautiful house.

"Who lives in that house?" he asked.

"O king," answered the servant, "the richest man in the country lives there. He gives the most wonderful feasts every day to his rich friends."

"And what does he do for the poor?" asked the king.

"Nothing," answered the servant.

The next day the king dressed himself in old ragged clothes and went to the house of the rich man. The rich man sat before his door.

"O great one," said the king, bowing low, "pray give me a little food and let me rest in your beautiful home. I am hungry and tired."

"Get away from here," said the rich man in a loud, angry voice. "Get away, or I will call my servants to beat you. I will have no beggars around my house."

The king turned sadly away.

The next day he again dressed in the old ragged clothes, but he covered them with a handsome cloak of silk trimmed with gold and jewels. Then he went once more to the home of the rich man.

As before, the rich man sat before his door. But as soon as he saw the stranger in the rich cloak he sprang to his feet and came to meet him.

Taking the stranger by the hand he led him into the house and soon had a wonderful feast spread before him.

"Eat, my friend," he said. "It is a great pleasure to have such a man as you enter my home."

The king took up some of the rich food and broke it into small pieces. But instead of eating any of them he put them into the folds of his rich cloak.

"Why do you not eat the food?" asked the rich man. "Why do you put it in your cloak?"

"Because it is my cloak you are feeding and not me," answered the king. "Yesterday I came to you dressed like a poor man and you drove me away. Today, because I have on this fine cloak, you make a feast for me. But I am the same today as yesterday—still your king."

As he said this the king rose, and, throwing back the rich cloak, stood dressed in the old ragged clothes.

"Forgive me! Forgive me, O king!" cried the rich man. "I have been proud and selfish. But from this day no poor man shall be driven from my door. You have taught me that a man is more than his clothes."

Adapted from Catherine T. Bryce. *Fables from Afar.* (N.Y.: Newson, 1910).

THE COUNTRY MOUSE AND
THE CITY MOUSE
A FABLE OF AESOP

Once a little mouse who lived in the country invited a little mouse from the city to visit him. When the city mouse sat down to dinner he was surprised to find that the country mouse had nothing to eat except barley and grain.

"Really," he said, "you do not live well at all; you should see how I live! I have all sorts of fine things to eat every day. You must come to visit me and see how nice it is to live in the city."

The country mouse was glad to do this, and after a while he went to the city to visit his friend.

The very first place that the city mouse took the country mouse to see was the kitchen cupboard of the house where he lived. There, on the lowest shelf behind some stone jars, stood a big paper bag of brown sugar. The little city mouse gnawed a hole in the bag and invited his friend to nibble for himself.

The two mice nibbled and nibbled, and the country mouse thought he had never tasted anything so delicious in his life. He was just thinking how lucky the city mouse was, when suddenly the door opened with a bang and in came the cook to get some flour.

"Run!" whispered the city mouse. And they ran as fast as they could to the little hole where they had come in. The country mouse was shaking all over when they got safely away, but the city mouse said, "That is nothing. She will soon go away and then we can go back."

After the cook had gone away and shut the door they stole softly back, and this time the city mouse had something new to show. He took the little country mouse into a corner on the top shelf where a big jar of dried prunes stood open. After much tugging and pulling they got a large dried prune out of the jar and onto the shelf. Then they began to nibble at it. This was even better than the brown sugar. The country mouse liked the taste so much that he could hardly nibble fast enough. But all at once, in the midst of their eating, there came a scratching at the door and a sharp, loud *miaouw!*

They ran as fast as they could to the hole.

The city mouse said, "That was the old cat. She is the best mouser in town. If she gets you, you are dead."

"This is terrible," said the little country mouse. "Let's not go back to the cupboard again."

"I'll tell you what," said the city mouse, "I will take you to the cellar. There is something special there."

Adapted from Sara Cone Bryant. *Stories to Tell to Children.* (Boston, MA: Houghton Mifflin, 1907).

So the city mouse took his little friend down the cellar stairs and into a big cupboard where there were many shelves. On the shelves were jars of butter and cheeses in bags and out of bags. Overhead hung bunches of sausages, and there were spicy apples in barrels standing about. It smelled so good that it went to the little country mouse's head. He ran along the shelf and nibbled at a cheese here and a bit of butter there, until he saw an especially rich, very delicious-smelling piece of cheese on a strange little stand in a corner. He was just on the point of putting his teeth into the cheese when the city mouse saw him.

"Stop! Stop!" cried the city mouse. "That's a trap!"

The country mouse stopped, and said, "What's a trap?"

"That thing is a trap," said the city mouse. "The minute you touch the cheese with your teeth something comes down on your head hard and you're dead."

The little country mouse looked at the trap; and he looked at the cheese; and he looked at the little city mouse. "If you'll excuse me," he said, "I think I'll go home. I'd rather have barley and grain to eat, and eat it in peace and comfort, than have brown sugar and dried prunes and cheese—and be frightened to death all the time!"

So the little country mouse went back to his home, and there he lived in peace all the rest of his life.

THE MISER
A MIDDLE EASTERN STORY

Once upon a time a kind old man and his wife had the misfortune to have a miser for a neighbor. When it was necessary for the old man and woman to borrow anything, they always had to return it with interest. If they borrowed one cup of sugar they returned two; if they borrowed a washcloth they returned a towel.

After a while the old wife grew tired of this. She decided to teach the miser a lesson. One day she asked him if he would lend her his big copper cooking pot. It was his best pot and the miser wasn't too happy.

"Our children and grandchildren are coming for supper," said the old woman, "and I haven't a pot big enough for the stew I'm making. Your copper cauldron would do fine. Perhaps sometime we might do you a favor."

So the miser handed over the copper cauldron. "You may borrow it," he grumbled, "but you know my rule."

"Yes," said the old woman, "I know. Thank you very much."

The next evening she returned the cauldron. On looking into it the miser was surprised to see at the bottom a nice little pewter saucepan.

"What's this?" he asked.

The old woman was surprised too. "I declare," she exclaimed, "the pot had a little one."

"It belongs to me," cried the miser quickly. "The pot is mine and its child is mine too."

"Very well," said the old woman. "I was going to pay you a bit for the use of the pot . . ."

"I'd rather keep the saucepan," the miser interrupted, for he could see that it was a valuable one.

A few weeks later the old woman again asked the miser to lend her his big cooking pot, which he did.

A day went by. Two days. A week. But the old woman did not return the pot. At last the miser could wait no longer and went off to her house. Without so much as a greeting he at once demanded his pot.

"Why haven't you returned it?" he asked angrily.

"I couldn't," said the old woman putting down her knitting.

"You couldn't? Why not?"

"I'm very sorry, but I have bad news for you. Your pot died."

The miser turned purple with rage. "What kind of nonsense is this?" he shouted. "Do you expect me to believe that a pot can die?"

Retold by Rose Dobbs. *More Once-Upon-a-Time-Stories* (N.Y.: Random House, 1961).

"Of course I do," said the old woman calmly. "If you believe that a pot can have a little one you'll just have to believe that a pot can die."

She took up her knitting, and the miser—muttering and grumbling—had no other choice but to leave.

HOW THE ROBIN'S BREAST BECAME RED

Long ago in the far north, where it is very cold, there was once upon a time a great, blazing fire. All day and all night a hunter and his little boy took care of it and kept it burning brightly. There was no other fire in the whole world, and the squirrels and the rabbits and the chipmunks crept near to warm their toes before they hurried away for their winter stores; and all the Indians came for coals that they might cook their food.

But one day the hunter became very ill, and so his son had to tend the fire alone. For days and days, and nights and nights, the boy bravely kept it burning, running off to the woods for twigs and hurrying back to toss them on to the blaze. At last he was too tired to keep his eyes open any longer. His head began to nod and he fell fast asleep on the ground.

In the deep woods of the northland lived a wicked old white bear. With his bright eyes he had been peering out from behind the pine trees and watching the fire. He hated all warm things, and he wished to put the fire out; but he was afraid of the hunter's sharp-pointed arrows. When the little boy closed his eyes the bear laughed to himself and began to step softly nearer, and nearer, and nearer the fire.

"Now is my chance!" he said. "We will have no fire in the northland."

Then he jumped on the logs with his big wet feet and trod on the coals, and tramped back and forth until he could not see a spark. Then he went back to his cave in the woods again, for he thought the fire was quite dead.

But up in a hemlock tree sat the little gray robin who lives in the northland; and she felt very sorry when she saw what the white bear had done. She fluttered down to the ground and over to the place where the fire had been, and she found—what do you think?—one tiny spark of flame that was still burning and one little red coal! Then the gray robin began hopping about, and flapping her little gray wings, and fanning the tiny spark to make it burn brighter. The red coal began to crackle, and the flames burned higher and higher until they scorched the poor robin's breast; but she never minded at all. She was so happy that the fire was beginning to blaze again.

When it was burning away cheerily once more, as if nothing had happened, the little boy awoke and the robin flew back to the hemlock tree; but the old white bear just growled and growled to think that the fire was safe.

But the robin, who had always been just a dull gray color all over, looked down where the flames had burned her breast, and it had turned a beautiful

Retold by Carolyn S. Bailey and Clara M. Lewis. *Favorite Stories for the Children's Hour* (N.Y.: Platt and Munk, 1965).

golden red. After that every gray robin had a red breast too, for the bird who kept the fire was the grandmother of them all.

The people in the northland love the robin very much indeed; and this is the story they tell of how the bird came to be called Robin Redbreast.

ARACHNE
A GREEK MYTH

Arachne was a beautiful maiden and the most wonderful weaver that ever lived. Her father was well known throughout the land for his great skill in coloring. He dyed Arachne's wools in all the colors of the rainbow. Since Arachne and her father lived far out in the countryside, she set her loom up outside so that she could be inspired by the birds, the flowers, and the sky.

People came from miles around to watch Arachne weave and to admire her work. They all agreed that the goddess Athena herself must have taught Arachne how to weave. But all the praise that Arachne had received went to her head. She proudly said that no one had taught her how to weave, and that not even Athena could weave more beautiful tapestries. Her father warned her not to compare herself to the goddess, but Arachne paid him no mind.

One day Arachne was putting the finishing touches on a new piece. As she worked she bragged of her skill to the many people that surrounded her loom. An old woman stepped forward to praise Arachne's tapestry.

"Your work is beautiful," said the old woman. "But do not be so bold as to claim that your work is better than Athena's."

Arachne just laughed at the old woman. "Go away, old woman. What do you know? If Athena's weavings are so beautiful, then I challenge her to a contest! If I lose I will gladly take the punishment, but Athena is afraid to weave with me."

Arachne had no sooner said these words than the old woman threw back her cloak and revealed that she was actually Athena in disguise. She said to Arachne, "Come, foolish girl, you shall have your contest!"

The people in the meadow surrounded the two women and the contest began. Both went quickly to work and for hours their shuttles flew swiftly in and out.

Athena, as usual, used the sky for her loom, and in it she wove a picture too beautiful to describe. Just look in the western sky each day when the sun sets and you will see an example of Athena's work.

Arachne was so sure of her skill that she had not been frightened by Athena's sudden appearance. Even Athena was amazed by the grace and beauty of Arachne's creation. But when Arachne lifted her eyes to Athena's work, she instantly knew that she had failed. She was so ashamed and so upset that anyone could weave better than she that she threw herself upon her loom and hid her face in the tapestry.

Athena took pity on her and said, "Your pride has brought you down, Arachne. But you shall continue to do the work for which you are best suited.

Retold by Martha Hamilton and Mitch Weiss—Beauty & the Beast Storytellers.

You shall be the mother of a great race which shall be called spiders. You and your children shall be among the greatest spinners and weavers on earth."

As she spoke, Arachne became smaller and smaller until she was scarcely larger than a fly.

From that day to this, Arachne and her family have been faithful spinners, but they do their work so quietly and in such dark places that very few people know what marvelous weavers they are.

THE JACKAL AND THE LION
A HINDU FOLK TALE

Once there was a great big jungle; and in the jungle there was a great big lion; and the lion was king of the jungle. Whenever he wanted anything to eat, all he had to do was to come up out of his cave in the stones and earth and *roar*. When he had roared a few times all the smaller animals of the jungle were so frightened that they came out of their holes and hiding places and ran this way and that to get away. Then, of course, the lion could see where they were. And he pounced on them, killed them, and gobbled them up.

He did this so often that at last there were no other animals left in the jungle except for one small jackal. The jackal had run away from the lion so many times that he was quite thin and very tired and couldn't run fast any more.

One day the lion came so near to the spot where the jackal was that the jackal thought, "I'm done for! The lion will surely catch me this time." But he used every bit of energy that he had and ran off so fast that all the lion could see was a big cloud of dust.

But at last came a day when the lion was so close to the jackal that he knew there was no chance for him to get away. Instead of running he walked right up to the lion as if he had meant to come all the time. When the lion saw him coming he roared in a terrible voice, "You miserable little creature, come here and be eaten at once! Why didn't you come to me before?"

The jackal bowed low to the ground. "Indeed, Your Honor, Father Lion, I meant to come before. I knew I ought to come before and I really wanted to come before. But every time I started to come, a dreadful great lion, a lion far bigger than you, came out of the woods and roared at me and frightened me so much that I ran away."

"What do you mean?" roared the lion. "There's no other lion in this jungle and you know it!"

Once again the jackal bowed low to the ground. "Indeed, Your Honor, Father Lion, I know that is what everyone thinks; but indeed there is another lion. And he is at least three times the size of you. His face is much more terrible and his roar far, far more dreadful. Oh, he is far more frightful than you are."

At that the lion stood up and roared so that the jungle shook.

"Take me to this lion," he said. "I'll eat him up and then I'll eat you up."

The little jackal danced on ahead and the lion stalked behind. The jackal led him to a place where there was a round, deep well of clear water. The jackal went on one side of the well and the lion strutted up to the other.

Adapted from Sara Cone Bryant. *Stories to Tell to Children* (Boston, MA: Houghton Mifflin, 1907).

"He lives down there, Your Honor, Father Lion; he lives down there!"

The lion came close and looked down into the water—and a lion's face looked back at him out of the water! The lion roared and shook his mane and showed his teeth. And the lion in the water shook *his* mane and showed *his* teeth. The lion above shook his mane again and growled again and made a terrible face. But the lion in the water made just as terrible a one back. The lion above couldn't stand that. He leaped down into the well after the other lion.

But, of course, as you know very well, there wasn't any other lion! It was only his reflection in the water!

So the poor old lion floundered about in the water, but he couldn't get up the steep sides of the well, and so he drowned.

The jackal, who was overjoyed, ran to spread the word; and soon other animals came once again to live in the jungle.

THE FOOLISH DRAGON
A TALE FROM CHINA

Long, long ago there lived a dragon in the great China sea. More than anything else in the world this dragon loved his wife. And he spent all his time granting her every wish.

One day he noticed that his wife was not looking well.

"What is it, my dear?" he asked. "What is troubling you?"

"I want something," answered she. "But I won't tell you what it is because I know you won't get it for me."

The dragon was hurt.

"Have I ever refused to get you what you want?" he asked. "Please tell me."

And he coaxed and begged so hard that at last his wife said, "I have heard that monkeys' hearts are delicious. I long to eat a monkey's heart. If I don't, I know I shall die."

The poor dragon was terrified at the thought of losing his wife. But a monkey's heart! How could he ever get that?

"You know the monkeys live high in the trees, deep in the forests. How could I ever reach them?" he said.

"There," said the wife, beginning to cry, "I knew you didn't mean it when you said you'd do anything for me. You don't really care for me at all. And now I shall surely die."

The dragon didn't know what to do. Finally he said to himself, "One can only try."

So he left the great China sea, went ashore, and journeyed until he came to a forest. There, way up in a tree, he spied a frisky monkey.

"Good afternoon, pretty one," he said sweetly. "That is a very tall tree you're in. Aren't you afraid you'll fall out?"

"Me—fall out of a tree!" The monkey burst out laughing. "Ha, ha, ha!" he laughed. "Who ever heard of such a thing?"

The dragon tried again. "That isn't a very juicy-looking tree," he said, more sweetly than before. "I know a forest full of trees laden with ripe, juicy fruit. It's only across the sea."

"You are indeed a foolish dragon," said the monkey. "What you say is all very well, but how would I cross the sea?"

"Why," said the dragon innocently, "all you have to do is get on my back and I'll swim across with you."

So the little monkey came down and climbed up on the dragon's back.

Retold by Rose Dobbs. *Once Upon a Time* (N.Y.: Random House, 1950).

The dragon, of course, lost no time in striking out for the China sea. When they were halfway across the dragon suddenly dived down beneath the water.

"Where are you going? What are you doing?" cried the monkey in alarm.

"I might as well tell you now," said the dragon. "There is no forest and no trees and no juicy fruit. There is only my wife who is ill and who says nothing but a monkey's heart will cure her. And so I am trying to drown you."

The monkey thought fast and quick. "My dear friend," he said, "why didn't you tell me before we started out? Gladly would I give up my heart to help your wife. But, don't you know that monkeys never carry their hearts around with them? I left mine in the tree where you found me. However, if you don't mind going back, I'll be happy to fetch it for you at once."

The dragon turned around and went back to the forest and the very tree where he had first seen the monkey. The little monkey, with a leap and a bound, was soon safe in the topmost branch.

The dragon waited and waited and begged and begged the monkey to come down with his heart. But the monkey didn't even bother to answer him. And for all I know that foolish dragon is still waiting there. Perhaps in time he will learn that monkeys carry with them not only their hearts but their clever thinking caps too.

HOW BROTHER RABBIT FOOLED WHALE AND ELEPHANT
AN AFRICAN-AMERICAN FOLK TALE

One day Brother Rabbit was running along on the sand when he saw Whale and Elephant talking together. Brother Rabbit crouched down and listened to what they were saying.

"You are the biggest thing on the land, Brother Elephant," said Whale, "and I am the biggest thing in the sea. If we join together we can rule all the animals in the world and have our way about everything."

"Very good, very good," trumpeted Elephant. "That suits me. We will do it."

Brother Rabbit snickered to himself. "They won't rule me," he said.

He ran away and got a very long, very strong rope, and he got his big drum and hid the drum a long way off in the bushes. Then he went along the beach till he came to Whale.

"Oh, please, dear strong Mr. Whale," he said, "will you do me a favor? My cow is stuck in the mud a quarter of a mile from here. And I can't pull her out. But you are so strong and so kind. Will you help me?"

Whale was so pleased with the compliment that at once he said, "Yes."

"Then," said Rabbit, "I will tie this end of my long rope to you, and I will run away and tie the other end round my cow, and when I am ready I will beat my big drum. When you hear that, pull very, very hard, for the cow is stuck very deep in the mud."

"Huh!" grunted Whale. "I'll pull her out even if she is stuck to the horns."

Brother Rabbit tied the rope end to Whale, and ran off till he came to the place where Elephant was.

"Oh please, mighty and kindly Elephant," he said, making a very low bow, "will you do me a favor?"

"What is it?" asked Elephant.

"My cow is stuck in the mud about a quarter of a mile from here," said little Brother Rabbit, "and I cannot pull her out. Of course you could. Won't you please help me?"

"Certainly," said Elephant grandly, "certainly."

"Then," said Brother Rabbit, "I will tie one end of this long rope to your trunk and the other to my cow, and as soon as I have tied her tightly I will beat my big drum. When you hear that, pull; pull as hard as you can, for my cow is very heavy."

"Never fear," said Elephant, "I could pull twenty cows."

Adapted from Sara Cone Bryant. *Stories to Tell to Children* (Boston, MA: Houghton Mifflin, 1907).

"I am sure you could," said Rabbit politely, "only be sure to begin gently and pull harder and harder till you get her."

Then he tied the end of the rope tightly round Elephant's trunk and ran away into the bushes. There he sat down and beat his big drum.

Whale began to pull, and Elephant began to pull, and in a jiffy the rope tightened till it was stretched as tight as could be.

"This is a remarkably heavy cow," said Elephant, "but I'll get her!" And he braced his forefeet in the earth and gave a tremendous pull.

"Dear me!" said Whale. "That cow must be stuck mighty tight," and he drove his tail deep in the water and gave a mighty pull.

He pulled harder; Elephant pulled harder. Pretty soon Whale found himself sliding toward the land. The reason was, of course, that Elephant had something solid to brace against. And, also, each time Elephant pulled the rope in a little, he took a turn with it around his trunk!

But when Whale found himself sliding toward the land, he was so angry with the cow that he dove head first down to the bottom of the sea. What a pull that was! Elephant was jerked off his feet, and came slipping and sliding to the beach and into the surf. He was terribly angry. He braced himself with all his might and pulled his best. At the pull Whale came up out of the water.

"Who is pulling me?" spouted Whale.

"Who is pulling me?" trumpeted Elephant.

And then each saw the rope in the other's hold.

"I'll teach you to play cow!" roared Elephant.

"I'll show you how to fool me!" fumed Whale.

And they began to pull again. But this time the rope broke. The Whale turned a somersault and the Elephant fell over backward.

At that, they were both so ashamed that neither would speak to the other. So that broke up the bargain between them.

And Brother Rabbit sat in the bushes and laughed, and laughed, and laughed.

THE SCORPION

Orion was one of the greatest of the Greek giants. Because he was the son of Poseidon, the god of the sea, he was as much at home in the water as on land. When he wished to get from one island to another he walked across on the bottom of the ocean. He was so tall that his head was always above the waves, and so large and broad that his travels caused high tides.

From childhood on, Orion was famous for his beauty and his tremendous strength. He grew up to be a great hunter, able to track and slay all kinds of beasts with the help of his giant hound Sirius. When the island of Chios was oppressed and terrified by lions and wolves, Orion came to its assistance. He tracked down and destroyed every one, so that the people and their flocks could live in safety.

By the time Orion came to the large island of Crete his fame was so great that Artemis, the goddess of the moon, invited him to go hunting with her. All went well until Orion, who had become vain of his skill, began to boast that he would soon have killed all the wild animals in Crete. Now a scorpion who was listening said to himself that this must not be. So he lay in wait for Orion and stung him to death with his poisoned tail.

But Orion's spirit did not have to go down to dwell in the Underworld with the souls of ordinary mortals. The gods, who loved him, transported him instead to the sky, where he can be seen in his golden armor and sword-belt, holding up his golden shield, and with his faithful dog, Sirius, at his heel. The scorpion who saved the wild animals of Crete was also raised into the heavens, and became a constellation in the southern sky.

Every night, as the Scorpion rises, Orion fades and vanishes.

Retold by Alison Lurie. *The Heavenly Zoo: Legends and Tales of the Stars* (N.Y.: Farrar, Straus and Giroux, 1979).

THE BAKER'S DAUGHTER
AN ENGLISH FOLK TALE

There was once a baker who had two daughters. Though they were twins, yet they were as different as summer and winter. One was generous and good-natured, while the other was selfish, greedy, and cross.

On a cold evening, when the wind swept the streets like a broom, the good-natured daughter was serving in the baker's shop. A poor ragged old woman came in leaning on a staff and asked if she might have a bit of dough. "Certainly, granny," said the girl, and she pulled off a large piece.

And might she bake it in the oven? asked the old woman.

"Yes, surely," said the baker's daughter.

The old woman sat in the corner and seemed to sleep until the bread was done. "Wake up, granny," said the girl. And then she cried out, "Why, look! The loaf has doubled in size."

"And so shall it always be for you because of your generous heart," said the old woman, who was really a fairy in disguise. She threw off her cloak and stood up all tall and shining, and touched the girl with her staff. And from that day on, every loaf of bread or cake or pie the baker's daughter put into the oven came out twice as large.

Time went on and one evening the ill-natured daughter was serving in the baker's shop. The same ragged old woman shuffled in leaning on her staff, and asked for a piece of dough. The girl grudgingly gave her a small bit, for her father had told her she must be kind to beggars.

And might she bake it in the oven? asked the old woman.

"Oh, very well, if you must," answered the baker's daughter.

So the old woman sat in the corner and seemed to sleep. When the bread was done, the baker's daughter opened the oven door and saw that the dough had doubled in size.

"That's too large for the likes of her," she said, and set the loaf aside for herself. She pulled off another piece of dough half the size of the first, and put it into the oven.

Presently the bread was done, and the baker's daughter opened the oven door and saw that the dough had swelled so that this loaf was twice the size of the first one. "That's far too large for the likes of her," she said, and set it aside with the other. Then she pulled off a tiny bit of dough, hardly as big as her thumb, and shoved it into the oven.

But when she opened the door again, the old woman's tiny bit of dough had swelled up so much it almost filled the oven, and it was all shiny with

Retold by Alison Lurie. *Clever Gretchen and Other Forgotten Folktales* (N.Y.: Crowell, 1980).

sugar and full of currants and raisins. "That's far too large and far too fine for the likes of her," said the baker's daughter, and she put the third loaf aside with the other two.

Now the old woman opened her eyes and sat up, and asked if her bread was done.

"It was burnt up in the oven, hoo-hoo," said the girl laughing.

"Is that all you have to say to me?" asked the old woman.

"Hoo-hoo, what else should I say?" cried the baker's daughter, laughing still.

"And so shall it always be for you," cried the fairy, and she threw off her cloak and stood up tall and shining. "Henceforth you shall say nothing else but *whooo-whoo.*"

She struck the baker's daughter with her staff, and the girl turned into an owl and flew out hooting into the night.

THE BRAVE WOMAN AND
THE FLYING HEAD

There was once a woman who traveled to a nearby village, her infant son strapped to a cradleboard on her back. She was bringing food to her relatives whose crops had not done well that season.

When she was deep in the forest she heard a terrible sound, the sound of trees being knocked down, the sound of a great wind coming in her direction. She looked back and there, far away, above the tree tops was a Flying Head.

Flying Heads were awful creatures, heads with no bodies—just long trailing hair and great paws like those of a bear. Those paws were forever grasping at anything within their reach, for the monsters were always hungry.

The woman knew the Flying Head would soon catch her scent, and so she quickly took the food from her pack and scattered it in every direction. She then began to run.

"Have courage," she whispered to her child. "I will not let this monster catch us."

Soon, just as the woman thought, the Flying Head caught the human scent. It swept through the forest following her trail until it came to the scattered food. There it stopped and began to eat, not willing to let even a single crumb escape its hungry mouth.

By the time it finished the last of the food the woman was far down the path, but the Flying Head was swift as the wind and soon took up the chase. Looking back over her shoulder as she ran, the woman saw the Flying Head close behind her, reaching out its big paws to grab her.

This woman had once heard a wise person say that the moccasin of a tiny child holds great power for good. So, quick as a wink she tossed one of her son's small shoes behind her into the monster's path.

The Flying Head grabbed with one big paw as the tiny moccasin fell, but missed, tangling its long hair in the brush which grew beside the path. Growling, it rolled into a patch of brambles where its long hair was caught. Meanwhile the woman, running as swift as a fox, continued down the path until she could run no further. Then she climbed up high into a tall white pine. "Be silent, my son," she whispered. "The monster will not find us here."

It was not long before the Flying Head untangled itself from the brambles. With a terrible roar it flew into the air following the woman's trail through the forest. Soon it came to the foot of the tree and sniffed about, confused because the human scent went no further.

Just then, high up in the top of the tree, the woman's small son reached

Retold by Joseph Bruchac. *Iroquois Stories* (Trumansburg, N.Y.: Crossing, 1985).

out one hand and knocked loose a tiny branch which fell down, down, down . . . and struck the Flying Head. "HAARNNH!" roared the Flying Head. "A porcupine dropped its quills on me!" In anger it struck the tree a blow which knocked loose a huge dead limb that fell right on the Flying Head and pinned it to the ground. While the monster struggled to get free, the woman climbed down from the pine tree and dashed off into the woods.

Now the woman's home was not far away and she ran and ran and ran and ran. Soon she reached the edge of her village and before her was the door of her lodge. She burst inside and fell down by the coals which still glowed from her cooking fire.

For a time she rested, feeling safe at last. Then, thinking that her child might be hungry, she looked around for something to eat. All that was left was a handful of chestnuts which she thrust into the fire to cook.

Meanwhile, the terrible Flying Head freed itself at last from the fallen limb. Filled with rage, it followed the trail of the woman right to the door of her lodge. It flew up and looked down through the smoke hole, ready to swoop in and grab her.

But when it looked down, what did the Flying Head see? It saw the woman reach into the fire, draw something out which looked to be a burning coal and thrust it into her mouth.

"Haarnnh," growled the monster, "she is eating fire. So fire is something good to eat!" It dove down right through the smoke hole and with both paws grabbed all the coals and shoved them deep into its mouth.

"Huunhhh?" it snarled as the fire started to burn within its belly.

"HAARRRNH!" it screamed as it flew out the smoke hole and was gone.

From that day on the village of the woman who was brave and did not lose her courage was never again bothered by the Flying Head.

THE SQUIRE'S BRIDE
A NORWEGIAN FOLK TALE

Once upon a time there was a squire who owned a large farm and had plenty of money in the bank. But there was one thing that he wanted, and that was a wife. He figured all he would have to do would be to choose someone, for any woman would be glad to marry a wealthy man like himself.

One day the daughter of a neighboring farmer was working for him in the hay field. The squire saw her and liked her very much, and since she was the child of poor parents he thought if he only hinted that he wanted to marry her that she would say yes at once. So he told her that he had been thinking of getting married again.

"That is very interesting, sir," replied the young woman, and she just kept right on raking the hay.

"Yes, I have decided to be married again. And you are the one I have chosen to be my wife."

"No, thank you all the same sir, but I am not ready to be married."

The squire was not used to being refused, and the more she refused him the more determined he was to marry her. Finally he sent for her father and told him that if he could talk with his daughter and arrange the marriage, the squire would forget about the money he had lent the father and would even give him a piece of land close to the meadow.

The father was very pleased with this offer. "Yes, you may be sure I'll bring my daughter to her senses. She is only a child, and doesn't know what's best for her."

But none of his coaxing or begging had any effect. She would not marry the squire, she said, even if he sat buried in gold up to his ears.

The squire waited day after day, but at last he became so angry and impatient that he told the poor farmer he had better arrange the marriage at once, if he expected the squire to stand by his promise.

The farmer could think of only one way out of the situation. He said to the squire, "Go ahead and get everything ready for the wedding. When all the wedding guests have arrived, send for my daughter. She'll assume you want her to do some work on your farm. But when she arrives, she'll be so impressed by all the beautiful bridal clothes and the number of guests that she'll agree to be married without taking the time to think it over.

The squire thought this was an excellent plan and set his servants to work at once. They prepared for the wedding in grand style. When the guests had arrived, the squire called one of his farm lads and told him to run down to his neighbor and ask him to send him what he had promised.

Adapted from P.C. Asbjornsen. *Fairy Tales from the Far North* (N.Y.: A.L. Burt, 1897).

The boy ran off and when he arrived at the neighbor's house he said to the farmer, "My master has sent me to bring back what you promised him, and there is no time to waste for he is terribly busy today."

"Yes, yes! Run down to the meadow and take her with you."

The boy ran to the meadow where he found the daughter raking hay, and said to her, "I am to fetch what your father has promised my master."

The young woman realized at once that they were trying to trick her, and so she said to the boy, "Why yes, it must be that bay mare of ours. You had better go and take her. The boy jumped on the back of the bay mare and rode home at full gallop, and ran to the squire's room.

"Have you got her with you?" asked the squire.

"She's down at the door," said the boy.

"Take her up to the room that used to be my mother's."

"But master," replied the boy, "she's very stubborn. I'm not sure I can manage that."

"Do as I tell you, and be quick about it! And if you can't manage her alone, then get some others to help you."

The boy took one look at the squire's red and angry face and knew it would be of no use to argue. So he ran to the barn and got all the farm hands to help him. It was no easy job. Some pulled at the head of the mare, while others pushed from behind; and at last they got her upstairs and into the room. The boy returned to the squire.

"She's upstairs at last, master. But it was a terrible job. It was the worst I have ever had to do on this farm!"

"Never mind your grumbling," said the squire. "Now send the women up to dress her."

"But master!"

"I said that's enough of your talk. Tell them to dress her and to be sure not to forget the veil or her flower wreath."

The boy ran to find the women. "Listen, the master is out of his mind. He wants you to go upstairs and dress the bay mare as a bride. I guess he wants to give the guests a good laugh."

So they dressed the horse as best they could in all the wedding finery, and then the boy ran to the squire and told him that everything was done just as he had instructed.

"Excellent, excellent," said the squire. "Now bring her down and I will receive her myself at the door."

There was a terrible clatter on the stairs as the bride was being led down. When the door opened and the squire's bride entered the room, everyone except the squire burst into laughter. The squire's face turned red and then white with rage. He stormed out of the room and was not seen again for the rest of the day.

You may be sure that he had had enough of that bride; and they say he never went courting again.

Index

ABOUT THE AUTHORS

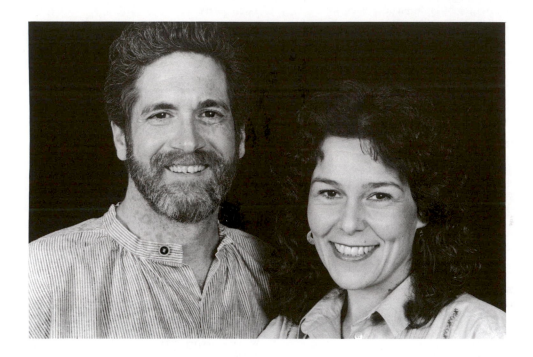

Martha Hamilton and Mitch Weiss, who live in Ithaca, New York, have been performing together professionally as Beauty & the Beast Storytellers at schools, libraries, coffeehouses, museums, festivals, and conferences throughout the United States and Canada since 1980. They leave it to their audiences to decide which one is the Beauty and which the Beast.

Using gesture, song, and physical movement in their performances this husband-and-wife team brings to life traditional folk tales from around the world, works by contemporary authors, and stories from their own experiences. Mitch is a natural comedian who can create an immediate rapport with any audience. Martha, with her expressive face and a penchant for telling poignant and moving tales, provides the perfect contrast. Their specialty is "tandem storytelling" where Mitch and Martha combine their differing styles, swapping lines and impersonating characters to add an absorbing dimension to their art.

Martha, formerly a reference librarian at Cornell University, began telling stories as a hobby after she mistakenly walked into a storytelling workshop while attending a library conference. She was eventually introduced to Mitch by a friend who told her, "Mitch may not know it, but he's a storyteller." Mitch had majored in government as a student at Cornell, a field which some have jokingly commented seems "perfect for a storyteller." At the time he was one of the owners/workers at the cooperatively run Moosewood Restaurant, an Ithaca landmark because of its best-selling vegetarian cookbook.

Mitch learned three stories in the first few days after he and Martha met, and now admits: "I haven't learned a story that fast since. It's amazing what love will make you do!" Although storytelling was merely a hobby when they first began, it soon became part of their livelihood as they cut their other jobs down to parttime. They have been fulltime professional storytellers since 1984.